NAVIGATING SOCIETAL CHANGE THROUGH DESIGN

Leading Missions for a Prosperous Future

Sara Gry Striegler and Julie Hjort

First published in Great Britain in 2025 by

Policy Press, an imprint of
Bristol University Press
University of Bristol
1–9 Old Park Hill
Bristol
BS2 8BB
UK
t: +44 (0)117 374 6645
e: bup-info@bristol.ac.uk

Details of international sales and distribution partners are available at
policy.bristoluniversitypress.co.uk

© Bristol University Press 2025

British Library Cataloguing in Publication Data
A catalogue record for this book is available from the British Library

ISBN 978-1-4473-7555-5 paperback
ISBN 978-1-4473-7556-2 ePub
ISBN 978-1-4473-7557-9 ePdf

The right of Sara Gry Striegler and Julie Hjort to be identified as authors of this work has been asserted by them in accordance with the Copyright, Designs and Patents Act 1988.

All rights reserved: no part of this publication may be reproduced, stored in a retrieval system, or transmitted in any form or by any means, electronic, mechanical, photocopying, recording, or otherwise without the prior permission of
Bristol University Press.

Every reasonable effort has been made to obtain permission to reproduce copyrighted material. If, however, anyone knows of an oversight, please contact the publisher.

The statements and opinions contained within this publication are solely those of the authors and not of the University of Bristol or Bristol University Press. The University of Bristol and Bristol University Press disclaim responsibility for any injury to persons or property resulting from any material published in this publication.

Bristol University Press and Policy Press work to counter discrimination on grounds of gender, race, disability, age and sexuality.

Cover design: Andy Ward
Front cover image: iStock/MaryliaDesign

One must still have chaos within oneself
to give birth to a dancing star.
                    Friedrich Nietzsche

Contents

List of figures and tables		vi
About the authors		vii
Thank you		ix
Preface		x
1	Five theoretical domains	1

Navigating a new story — 15

2	The imagination crisis	17
3	A preferred future	45

Navigating balance — 55

4	Holding the tension between opposing attitudes	57
5	Missions: balancing top-down and bottom-up	74

Navigating experiments — 95

6	Untying the knot through experiments	97
7	Learning through hypothesis	109

Navigating interdependence — 137

8	Weaving new patterns collectively	139
9	Building coalitions	153
10	Closing and opening	177

References	182
Index	193

List of figures and tables

Figures

1.1	Span of design disciplines	4
2.1	Boxing Future Health matrix	38
4.1	Opposing attitudes	58
4.2	Double diamond	64
4.3	The Systemic Design Framework	65
4.4	The Three Horizons Framework	71
5.1	The Megaphone Model	78
5.2	Innovation Fund Denmark's impact framework for mission-oriented innovation	90
6.1	Deep seriousness versus deep playfulness	106
7.1	Harvesting Learning Model	116
7.2	Breaking down the learnings: from foster care to adulthood	121
7.3	The Learning Framework's Five Elements, an adaptation	126
9.1	Outsiders and insiders	160
9.2	Place layers	170

Tables

2.1	Tame problems versus wicked problems	24
5.1	Traditional innovation versus mission-oriented innovation	80

About the authors

Sara Gry Striegler is the founder of Kindred Lab for Transitions, helping leaders and organizations navigate change, bridge sectors, and shape sustainable futures. Her work builds on leadership roles as Chief Executive Officer at Nordic Health Lab, where she connected the public healthcare system and private companies to co-create new solutions, and as Director for Societal Transitions at the Danish Design Center, pioneering futures design and mission-oriented innovation.

Sara is internationally recognized and part of the Top 50 World Economic Forum & Apolitical list of Most Influential People Revolutionising Governance in the Futures Thinking category (2020).

She is an experienced speaker and author of a chapter on mission-oriented innovation in Sigge Winther Nielsen's anthology on wicked problems (2023), a chapter in the book *Leadership of Public Innovation* (published in September 2022 in Danish), as well as *Strategic Innovation in Healthcare* (February 2020 in Danish).

Sara is Chair at the Social Innovation Academy and former external lecturer at Technical University of Denmark.

She holds an MSc in Engineering (Design Engineer) from the Technical University of Denmark and an executive education in Scenario Planning and Foresight from Oxford University and Saïd Business School.

Julie Hjort is the Chief Operating Officer at the Danish Design Center and has spearheaded the Center's mission to accelerate the transition to a circular economy. She has been a driving force in developing a design-based approach to mission-oriented innovation that she has applied both at the Danish Design Center and in external partnerships to tackle sustainability challenges. For over a decade, Julie has worked with design, innovation, leadership and transformation in interdisciplinary and public/private partnerships.

Julie is Chair at Maker, an association for physical entrepreneurship that runs an urban prototyping lab in Copenhagen. She is a seasoned speaker on the topic of circular transformation and mission-oriented innovation. Julie was profiled as a prominent circular designer by the Ellen MacArthur Foundation (fall 2023). Julie holds an MA in Contemporary Culture and Dissemination from the University of Copenhagen.

Thank you

We have spoken about this book with excitement, dreamed about it, laughed and cried over it, and, honestly, it has been a long time in the making. But the seed of this idea would never have been planted without the immense inspiration of Christian Bason. His relentless curiosity and insistence that our knowledge, work and insights are worth sharing have been a true driving force for us.

Our dear and wise friend Sara Solveig Ørnsholt, with her piercing X-ray vision, pinpointed areas of implicitness and critical yet constructive feedback, helped us refine the final product.

We are deeply grateful for the challenging questions and enthusiastic cheering from both Sidsel Winther and Gry Brostrøm in their role as our wing-women. This balance of critical inquiry and heartfelt encouragement has been invaluable throughout these many years of tackling complex problems, leadership and systemic change.

Oskar Stokholm Østergaard, the magnificent mind, has played a pivotal role in recalibrating our perspectives when needed and challenging our assumptions about the world. He has encouraged us to avoid the predictable route and to continue playing and experimenting.

Maria Arndt, who has helped us see how nerdy and complex ideas can be made accessible to many more people.

Ulrik Schøitz, who has posed the right questions – sometimes frustrating – but always pushing us to be intentional and courageous in our decisions.

Finally, a heartfelt thought and gratitude to our supportive families – Eva and Leif for their life wisdom and unwavering support, and to our respective partners, Mikkel and Mads, for their patience and forbearance during countless conversations, both big and small, about this book.

Preface

The blue light from the television fills the dark room, casting its fluorescent glow on our pale, weary faces. It is Sunday evening in October, and my husband and I are bracing ourselves for a new week ahead. It is my daughter's eighth birthday, and she and her elder brother sleep soundly after a long day of birthday celebrations. I sit on the sofa as the steady-toned journalist moves to the next headline in her list of the day's highlights.
14,500.
Fourteen thousand five hundred.
14,500 care workers who, each day, take on vital tasks in our healthcare system. Day after day, they provide care. Bathing your mother or father, tending to wounds, administering medicine, helping people restore physical abilities that have been lost. But beyond that, they offer something far more profound: the reassurance that we can live with dignity, comfort, and meaning.
14,500.
Fourteen thousand five hundred *short*.
This evening, Denmark's national broadcaster, Danmarks Radio, reports that if the new health reform is implemented, Denmark will lack 14,500 healthcare assistants needed to maintain services for the country's population by 2035. The heightened political focus following the health reform proposal of autumn 2024 has caused the media to intensify their coverage of the pressing issues that expose the growing cracks in our society.

This news feature is not an isolated case, nor is this a problem confined to healthcare. We lack police officers, we lack pedagogues, we lack prison guards, we lack teachers.

This recruitment problem indeed poses enormous challenges for our society, leading to significant consequences for kids, young people, older people, you, and us, the people these systems are supposed to support. Consequences that we are already witnessing the effects of today.

But is the problem merely a shortage of hands? Is there a need for more people in the care sector, the police force, the justice system and schools? And is the answer simply to educate more people into these domains?

What if it is our *assumptions* about the welfare state that needs rethinking? What if we are so blinded by the understandings and logics of yesterday that we cannot see what lies right in front of us tomorrow? What if this crisis is about much more than just recruitment, education and workforce shortages? What if it is about how we perceive and value care work, our linear approach to retirement, and the transactional nature of our current welfare model?

These kinds of projections about our future challenges are not new. They have been repeated several times in the broader media landscape. But as we fail to solve the challenges, the consequences become increasingly pronounced.

The recruitment crisis is one of many complex problems tied closely to other crises. And more are piling up. We see conflicts accelerating across society, echoing across borders worldwide. Societies are fracturing with widening divides between generations, genders and social groups, steadily propelling polarization. Every week brings new updates on devastating floods and hurricanes that wipe out cities. And each month marks yet another record as the hottest to date, testifying to the seriousness of climate change. Misinformation and disinformation increasingly permeate our daily lives. And widespread loneliness reaches across all layers of society. These challenges have a common nature: they are complex, interconnected and unruly. While we understand the gravity of these problems, we remain stuck.

It is no surprise that this leaves many with the question: Is it too late? Could it all collapse? Will our societies, as we know them, crumble to dust? Will chaos follow?

In this gloom, a pressing question arises: Can new logics, models, and solutions emerge from the ruins of our society?

Right there in my living room, my zombie-like state is interrupted by a surge of energy, as if I am stirred awake by the frustration and determination sparked by the news feature. I snap a photo, send it to Julie, and type, 'Argh. Over and over. Again. We must create a new narrative! And stop singing the same old song. [exploding head emoji].'

Glimpses of hope

Thankfully, our frustration is not only filled with dissatisfaction, uncertainty and disappointment. Right in the middle of that frustration burns the motivation to write this book, and it burns with a bright light. Over the past ten years, we, Julie and Sara, have experienced small pockets of change – glimpses of progress, where we move forward instead of feeling stuck. Our mission is to gather and demonstrate this with practical, concrete examples so that many more can access the knowledge and learnings we, along with innovators from around the world, have acquired. We aim to draw connections between many small opportunity spaces, ideas and disciplines to form a stronger foundation for creating the change so many long for.

With this book, we want to show that what may seem impossible and out of reach on the surface is, in fact, possible and right in front of us.

The nature of these societal challenges appears untameable and wild. We cannot define and isolate them as problems. We cannot analyse our way through them to completely understand them. It is simply not possible. Instead, we insist that we need to discover new paths. Not by remaining in analysis mode, because if we do, we will still be at it 100 years from now. No, we need to intervene. We must act and experiment to understand better and influence today's problems. As Design Professor Ida Engholm bluntly puts it: 'We face great challenges, but it is my claim that we do not need more knowledge about them. We need action' (Engholm, 2023).

In *Navigating Societal Change through Design*, we encourage the reader to venture into unknown territory and embrace uncertainty and the reality of not knowing the answers in advance. Together, we may create more glimpses of change, a better common language for facilitating transitions, and a greater willingness to experiment, play and learn. To do so, we need something to navigate by: we need navigating points.

Dreaming of this book

> In the eyes of the world, to dare is dangerous. For one might lose.
> And so, not daring is wise.
> Yet oh, how easily one may lose by not daring at all, what, though risked in daring,
> is rarely truly lost —and never so swiftly, so completely, as if it were nothing at all: one's very self.
>
> Kirkegaard (1849: 150)

With this book, we speak to multiple landscapes of actors representing different perspectives, knowledge, cultures, powers and logics.

On the one hand, we seek to spark enthusiasm and a rebellious spirit in policy actors, public bodies, private corporations and non-governmental organizations *within* the established system, helping them channel their frustration and drive for change.

On the other hand, we want to equip *outsiders*, be it think tanks, philanthropic organizations or innovators, with a deeper understanding of the system and identify crucial points that may help turn the system into something better.

We also wish to touch those sitting quietly in meetings, intuitively resenting what is going on but without the vocabulary to adequately express their concern. Or those who are frustrated and impatient and do not know what the first steps should be or which next move to make. Finally, we address those already active in transition work but who want to make an even more profound impact with their work.

We intend to give people a voice to express things they might already know but need a language and practice for. We hope it will encourage more people to test different perspectives, approaches and thinking in their own surroundings.

As Kierkegaard put it back in 1849, we will most likely lose our footing for a moment, but this should not keep us from moving on. We dream that the reader will experience courage, faith and, most importantly, agency towards shaping a better future. We, Sara and Julie, are doing this, personally, for Le and Bjørn – the two kids sleeping in their beds on that dark October night. For

Maximillian and Sebastian sleeping peacefully in their beds in the other part of the city. For all children across the globe. For the sake of their children and their children's future. For future generations and for the planet we inhabit.

How to read this book

The book comprises our experience and learning, developed over several years in close collaboration with dedicated colleagues and curious partners. Our knowledge primarily derives from exploration within *social transitions* – healthcare, youth, eldercare, policy making – and *sustainable transitions* – circular transition, green strategies, ecosystem collaboration and behavioural change. We draw on our previously written texts and cases, insights from experts and thinkers who have inspired us. We attempt to weave much of what we have learned from practice into an overview, which will inspire, provoke and offer new perspectives that lead to action. We bring it all together to provide four navigation points to navigate by in the wilderness of tackling societal challenges.

Through a *design lens*, this book connects the dots between these different professional domains: *mission-oriented innovation, futures design and strategic foresight, system innovation* and *leadership*. As we reach across the various disciplines, we aim to discover new connections. This decision to span broadly effectively leads to a multitude of exclusions. Our theoretical overview will be mainly introductory. We encourage the reader to explore further reading and follow the traces on some of the thinkers and practitioners we have been inspired by that have piqued our own appetite (see Acknowledgements).

As you move through the book, you will recognize that it is a practice-oriented book, blending methodology, expert input and theory, frameworks, and practical case examples from around the world.

Pathfinders

We target the book to a broad audience of professionals who work to influence complex and systemic societal challenges. We introduce a new role for these leaders and innovators who take action – we call them *pathfinders*. In our view, the pathfinder is vital in a wide range of functions, whether as individuals or connected to policy, industry, civic society or education. It is not *one role* with a conclusive list of traits. Instead, it describes a way of approaching entangled systemic challenges with a creative and persistent mindset insisting that change is possible.

Through the four navigation points, we share questions, reflections and examples of how design can feed systems change, making it applicable and practical for the reader to translate into her own context.

The four navigation points are:

- *Navigating a New Story*: on the power of imagination and storytelling to create a new direction.
- *Navigating Balance*: balancing the tension between different attitudes of time, scale and mindset.
- *Navigating Experiments*: exploring, learning and creating progress continuously through iterative experiments.
- *Navigating Interdependence*: understanding, embracing and making the space for interdependence and collaborations in new types of partnerships.

The four navigation points are interconnected but not necessarily sequential. Each offers examples, perspectives and approaches to tackling complex challenges. They function as waypoints you can chart on your nautical map, guiding you as you seek your course through uncharted waters.

1

Five theoretical domains

As a primer to the book's four navigating points, we briefly introduce the five theoretical domains that we base our practice on and refer to throughout the book.

We are practitioners, not academics, and our practice is based on a sometimes haphazard process of piecing together bits of theory, methodology and thinking from across different disciplines and compiling them in a patchwork way of working. The domains we share here are academic fields we keep bumping into that continue to challenge and inspire us so we can convert the thinking into practice. In some academics' opinion, our way of working and applying theory may come off as a bit messy, as we pragmatically and agnostically apply and adapt to whatever works in the specific context.

We are, however, biased when it comes to the design domain. As two designers, one by education and another by practice, we have a special connection to this domain. It is the offset for our practice and the professional lens from which we explore and gain inspiration from other theoretical domains.

The domains are the following:

- *Design*: Design is the intentional process of creating concepts, solutions, objects, systems, or experiences with a specific purpose or function in mind.
- *Mission-oriented innovation*: an economic and political new paradigm that puts solving societal challenges at the heart of innovation and collaboration across society.

- *Strategic foresight and futures design*: a way of thinking and working continuously to bring the future into the present, challenge the status quo, and expand our perspective.
- *System innovation*: a professional field that, to us, provides a theoretical framework and poses questions that help us understand the systems we are part of so we can better intervene in them.
- *Leadership*: a new way of thinking about leadership and followership, about power and how to distribute it, to mobilize actors to work together towards societal change.

We have chosen these five specific domains because, often tied together in different constellations, they have previously excelled as inspiring and valuable perspectives for us. Throughout the four navigation points of the book, we weave them together.

We will introduce these domains by focusing on how we understand them and what we can learn from them in light of the four navigation points. We will encourage and guide you towards further exploration of the domains. All the theoretical domains are intriguing academic fields to dig deeper into for curious readers.

This overview of the five domains also serves as a reference work you can circle back to as you read the book. If you consider yourself well-versed in these domains, then jump right to the first navigation point, *Navigating a New Story*.

On design

Everyone designs who devises courses of action aimed at changing existing situations into preferred ones. (Simon, 1969)

What is design?

In the past century, the field of design has been one of the strongest driving forces and methods for developing visual communication and industrial products in the private sector. In the last 20–25 years, however, design as a profession has 'splintered' and expanded to include the design of services, digital solutions, experiences, and new business and governance models in both the public and social sectors.

Design in this sense is both a noun – *a design* – referring to a product, a garment, a chair or a surgical instrument that is designed, and a verb *to design* that refers to the creation process leading up to new solutions.

Today, the design field includes methods and thinking that can be activated for transformation and change across companies, institutions, agencies and ministries. As part of this expansion in design, we have witnessed the growth of new design branches such as design for social innovation (Manzini, 2015), system design (Leadbeater and Winhall, 2020), transition design (Fry, 2007), bio designs (Myers, 2014), mission-oriented design (DDC, 2021) and even planetary design (Engholm, 2023).

We would like to highlight *transition design*, as it is a design approach aimed at guiding society through large-scale transitions towards more sustainable, resilient and just futures. Transition design acknowledges that we are living in 'transitional times' and takes as its central premise the need for societal transitions to build more sustainable futures with the belief that design has a crucial role to play in these transitions. At its core, transition design emphasizes rethinking systems and behaviours (Irwin et al, 2015).

The broad range of design disciplines is visualized in Figure 1.1. It depicts how the design application varies, depending on what we design. In this book, our focus lies on the right-hand side of the model as we delve into the design practice of societal change processes. However, the cross-cutting horizontal lines indicate that several design disciplines apply across the spectrum. System designers, for example, draw on elements from information design and product design, navigating between the abstract use of design as a process and the tangible use of design as form.

The different design disciplines vary depending on their specific context and craft; for example, industrial designers are trained differently than system designers. However, some *core characteristics* define the application of design that cuts across all the disciplines. These are:

- *To be explorative and challenge assumptions.* Designers will try to understand the nature of a problem or an opportunity before searching for its solution.

Figure 1.1: Span of design disciplines

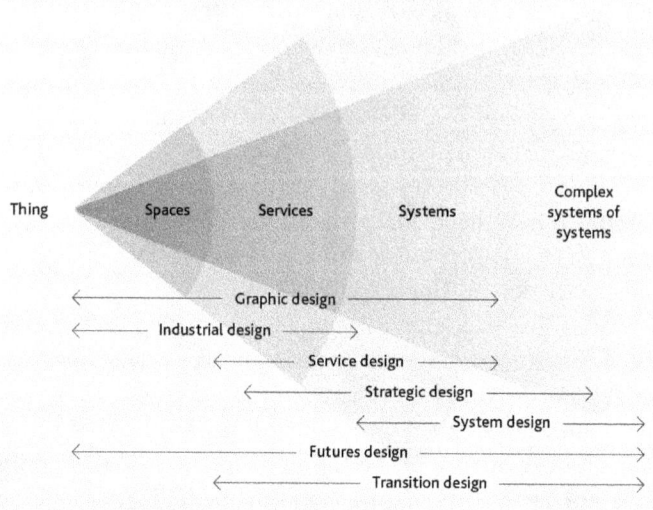

Source: Adapted from Hill and Melander (2025)

- *To bring empathy into play.* The design practice focuses on what drives people's behaviour in their specific context, trying to uncover their explicit, unspoken and undiscovered needs.
- *To experiment.* The design process is based on iterative prototyping. It is central to the designer's mindset to be in a constant flux between an exploratory and a propositional state, where insights emerge through the continuous process of exploring problems or opportunities and attempting to intervene in them through practical prototyping.
- *To make the future concrete.* Designers use tangible prototypes: prompts, mock-ups and visual aids to facilitate exploration, processes, dialogue and collaboration.

A vital characteristic not applicable to all design disciplines but relevant for many designers is that the design process is engaging. Design provides powerful tools for the involvement of people (citizens, end users, employees and partners), enabling more to contribute, gain insights and, ultimately, in some cases, change their practice to implement new solutions.

Who is the designer?

We began with the famous Nobel Prize-winning economist Herbert Simon, who claims that anyone can design by intentionally creating change through actions that lead from a current state to a desired one. This statement resonates with the recognized design academic and honorary professor Ezio Manzini, who suggests that design as a discipline should not be reserved for the relatively small group of professionally trained designers. He distinguishes between *diffuse* design and *expert* design, explaining how everybody designs through their everyday interactions and activities, where expert design performed by professional designers plays a crucial role in guiding these diffuse processes by providing the tools and frameworks needed for change (Manzini, 2015).

Equally to Manzini's perspectives, we suggest that *all* people may consider themselves designers. The people who undertake societal change processes, the pathfinders we address in this book, may benefit substantially from borrowing from and utilizing practices from design. We do not mean to discredit professionally trained designers here. They are crucial in building the capacity for transition across society. But the designerly way of navigating societal change should not be limited to a small group with a specific professional background. Therefore, this book invites many more people to utilize design in their practice.

As we connected with designer and systems thinker Jennie Winhall, she reflected on the word 'designer'. She responded: 'I probably use design as a bit of a shorthand to describe an act of creation.' Winhall's reflection resonates with us. In our view, the core characteristics of design for societal change sum up to a creative mode, a way of being that enables people to challenge, understand, test, intervene and create something that can provide practical stepping stones for us to move forward into new and better systems. These creative traits are vital and, in our view, somewhat underutilized and undervalued in society today.

A design lens on new theoretical domains

Being designers, we are keen to explore how design can connect the different theoretical domains. We think of the design perspective as a methodical and practice-oriented *how to* approach the other fields. We also explore new practices that emerge in the interface between the different domains. Through the book, we will see how the realm of design today influences and inspires the other domains and how the design field, accordingly, is challenged to adapt and evolve through its interaction with these new ways of thinking and working.

Let us introduce the four other theoretical domains we manoeuvre within the book.

On mission-oriented innovation

Over the past five years, *mission-oriented innovation* has gained footing as a distinctive new approach to solving complex challenges. The concept of mission-oriented innovation was coined by Professor Mariana Mazzucato at University College London's Institute for Innovation and Public Purpose.

With her 2011 book, *The Entrepreneurial State*, Mazzucato prepared the ground for a new role for the state to increasingly and more proactively catalyse innovation, shape new markets and drive public value creation around societal challenges. While Mazzucato's economic framework is novel, her thinking builds on the historical analysis of financial success in the United States, recognizing how the United States as an entrepreneurial state has been the primary risk taker in driving technological innovation, for example, through the US National Science Foundation (Mazzucato, 2018a).

Through her body of work, Mazzucato argues that we must rethink the role of government in society, putting public purpose first in how states operate. She brings forward the US moon landing in 1969 as an example of a mission. It was a clear, inspiring, bold ambition with a concrete timeline: to land on the moon within the century. Mazzucato argues how the moon landing laid the ground for cross-disciplinary, cross-sectoral and cross-actor innovation, which was equally beneficial to society as the moon landing itself. For instance, it led to the development of the microchip and Teflon material, which is still widely used almost 60 years later (Mazzucato, 2018b).

Mazzucato's ideas and theoretical framework were adopted by the European Union (EU), which led to the launch of five EU missions in September 2021 targeting challenges and setting ambitious goals for the EU to be achieved within health, climate and the environment by 2040. Through the Horizon Europe programme, €673.24 million was dedicated to rolling out the EU missions through research and innovation.

Along with the EU and Institute of Innovation and Public Purpose led by Mazzucato, the Organisation for Economic Co-operation and Development (OECD) has actively supported nations in implementing mission-oriented innovation in practice.

Today, we see the rise of several new missions emanating from various countries from different layers and perspectives in society. For example, national industrial or innovation strategies in Germany, the UK and Denmark; purpose-led missions in science, technology and innovation in the United States and in the UK; research-led missions in Trondheim, Norway and Limerick in Ireland; place-based-missions in Barcelona, Helsinki and Camden; and design-led missions in Sweden, Vinnova and in Denmark at the Danish Design Center (DDC).

The missions mentioned here vary immensely depending on the nature of the challenge they aim to tackle and, on each mission's respective owner and initiator. There are many formulas for how to *do missions*. Yet, some consistent features cut through almost all missions: Missions target defined impacts within a concrete societal challenge. They are bold, inspirational and widely relevant to society. With missions, it is acknowledged that no singular solution or investment will help the actors reach the goal. Instead, it is achieved by myriad solutions and activities driving cross-sectoral and bottom-up collaboration across several societal actors.

Mazzucato argues that missions should be clearly framed, measurable and time-bound, describing tangible effects such as reduced CO_2 emissions or waste, increased clean water, or improved human health, where the effects can be quantitatively measured. Yet we also see the rise of missions such as Vinnova's mission to 'ensure that every street in Sweden is healthy, sustainable and vibrant by 2030'. Here, the targeted impact is based on a more qualitative interpretation, for example, 'a vibrant street'. This is the case with the Norwegian mission 'From Youth to Young Adulthood' (KS, 2022) which tackles youths' social exclusion by building a new narrative around the preferred future.

Some organizations and people argue for more explorative targets, recognizing that the nature of the specific challenge may change over time, and the targets will change accordingly.

Design-led missions

With Mazzucato's ideas, mission-oriented innovation was largely introduced as a political and economic theoretical framework that elaborated on the *why* of mission-oriented innovation and, to a lesser extent, described the *how* of missions: how to practically translate this new political and economic paradigm into methodology and a new practice. Alongside pioneers such as Dan Hill and Vinnova, the DDC has been a playground for developing a design-driven approach to mission-oriented innovation. The DDC has described how design offers ways to navigate the explorative balance of bottom-up experimentation within the confines of a clear-cut mission statement (DDC, 2021).

On futures design and strategic foresight

Here, we describe the many different disciplines and practices that proactively engage with and try to learn from different outcomes of the future. This domain is pieced together by theory and thinking from across fields such as trend analysis, strategy development, business innovation and design.

Futures design is an approach that focuses on exploring and shaping potential future scenarios, often intending to address complex societal challenges or anticipate changes in technology, culture or the environment. It involves speculative thinking, scenario building and strategic foresight to imagine what the world might look like in the future and how design can influence or respond to these potential outcomes. Aspects of futures design include:

Five theoretical domains

- *Speculative design*: Focuses on exploring what-if questions by creating provocative and imaginative representations of possible futures. In their book, *Speculative Everything*, Anthony Dunne and Fiona Raby argue that speculative design challenges assumptions about the present and offers alternative visions of the future by raising critical questions about technology, society and culture, and, hence, encouraging debate and reflection (Dunne and Raby, 2013). Speculative design involves creating conceptual designs that challenge current assumptions or norms.
- *Strategic foresight*: The work with foresight originates in scenario planning, a discipline that arose from the need for organizations to survive and thrive in an increasingly global and connected world. Scenario planning, or strategic foresight, has seen increasing and steady progress since the 1950s due to significant and partly unforeseen and disruptive social crises that challenged our trust in society and our security (Ramirez and Wilkinson, 2016). Following the Second World War, US military strategist Herman Kahn developed scenarios to understand the possible outcomes of nuclear warfare. Traditional planning, including trend analysis and projections, were not sufficient tools for navigating the societal and environmental conditions: situations that change rapidly are of a hitherto unknown nature and full of ambiguity (Ramirez and Wilkinson, 2016). We can turn to Professor of Practice Rafael Ramirez and Professor Trudi Lang from Saïd Business School and the University of Oxford and their decades of expert knowledge and experience in scenario planning and strategic foresight to learn more.
- *Scenario development* or scenario planning creates multiple possible futures, exploring desirable and undesirable outcomes. It often entails building concrete and plausible future scenarios, analysing the changes that may occur in the future, and informing the decisions made in the present.

There are various tools and approaches for developing scenarios, but what they have in common is that they aim to mobilize our imagination and provide us with images of what alternative future outcomes could look like. They do not predict the future. Instead, future scenarios help to understand challenges and potentials in, for example, 20, 30 or 40 years.

The methods and utilization of strategic foresight and scenario planning are not new. It is a recognized method at the highest political levels: Australia started by exploring strategic foresight in 1985, and Canada adopted it in the 1990s. The Finnish Parliament's Committee on the Future was founded in 1993 to serve as a think tank for future science and technology policy in Finland, with a mission to create a dialogue with the government regarding critical future challenges and opportunities (Kimbell and Vesnic-Alujevic, 2020). Moreover, the UK Government Office for Science has published foresight on topics dating back to 2003.

In the late 1980s, the European Commission Joint Research Centre began applying strategic foresight in their work, which led to the development of the concept of 'anticipatory governance', and produced a series of reports for the future of Europe (European Commission Joint Research Centre, 2018). The OECD's Lab for Public Sector Innovation, which advises and supports governments in using new approaches to achieve political priorities, has also adopted anticipatory governance. This proactive approach integrates foresight, innovation and continuous learning into the heart of public governance (OECD, 2019).

Influence by design

Designers apply visual, concrete and collaborative methods to strategic foresight and scenario development, which makes it possible to explore and engage with the future jointly. In contrast to strategic foresight, which traditionally results in a report and is targeted at stakeholders with a certain level of abstraction and decision-making power, design-based approaches focus more on democratizing processes and distributing power. Several organizations have been exploring scenarios with design, for example, SuperFlux, Manyone (formerly Bespoke) and DDC.

The work often includes collaborating with various stakeholders to ensure diverse perspectives. The design approach enables people to identify new opportunities together with colleagues, users and partners. It provokes and inspires new dialogue and practices across actors, power structures, professions and organizations.

On system innovation

The scope of this book is to help pathfinders in the task of driving societal change, navigating in a context of complexity and uncertainty. Of course, the complex nature of societal challenges affects how we understand them and try to solve them. Thus, working with societal change demands that we take a systems approach and try to understand the structures, logics and values – within which our current challenges thrive. System innovation as a theoretical domain provides us with mental models we can draw from as we analyse systems and assess how to intervene in them.

We must underline that when we refer to systems, we do not suggest they can ever be fully grasped, contained or controlled. Systems are dynamic and effectively out of our control. However, as we learn about the mechanisms that maintain or drive systems forward, we can build up our capacity to initiate strategic interventions that potentially have broader systemic effects.

In this book, we have pieced together our understanding of system innovation by following the work of Donella Meadows (environmental theory), Charles Leadbeater (social innovation), Jennie Winhall (design and social innovation), Dan Hill (design and urban transformation) and Geoff Mulgan (policy and social innovation). We bring forward their voices and ideas in the book. However, we stress that the field is much larger and has ties to many academic disciplines, from psychology to computer technology.

We lean on environmentalist and system thinker Donella Meadows to describe a system. She defines a system as 'a set of things – people, cells, molecules, or whatever – interconnected in such a way that they produce their pattern of behaviour over time' (Meadows, 2008: 2). Her body of work emphasizes the dynamic nature and interconnectedness of systems, and she helps us create a vocabulary for analysing, and thus, intervening in them.

Meadows introduces vital concepts such as *feedback loops*, which are mechanisms that determine how a system regulates itself. Positive feedback loops reinforce or amplify a particular behaviour in the system. An example from biology is contractions during the process of birth that become more frequent and intense as the uterus contracts to expand the cervix, in order to give birth. In contrast, negative feedback loops counterbalance specific behaviour with a new kind of behaviour to maintain stability. Picture, here, how the body's temperature automatically regulates itself: when body temperature increases, we start sweating, which brings down the temperature. The idea of feedback loops and their interplay may help us analyse why specific actions in systems tend to lead to specific reactions. Accordingly, this knowledge can aid us in responding with targeted interventions.

With the notion of *leverage points*, Meadows describes 12 levers or places in the system where a slight shift in one thing can potentially produce significant changes across the system. The image of the *lever* helps us visually imagine a handle we might pull or push to cause further systemic change elsewhere in the system. She ranks these leverage points according to their effectiveness, where the least effective are levers such as changes in parameters, numbers or material flows, and the most effective levers are about changing the goals, mindsets and power to transcend paradigms (Meadows, 1999).

We see the ideas of leverage points reflected in Charles Leadbeater and Jennie Winhall's notion of systems change with their *Four Keys* that we introduce in the first navigation point as a backdrop for how we might unlock systems and work within them (Leadbeater and Winhall, 2020).

On leadership

The protagonist of this book is the person who takes on the tough but meaningful role as pathfinder, committing herself to navigate in societal change processes and to mobilize systems change.

Throughout the book we continuously add new levels of complexity to this role: she should be able to set a direction of an alternative future, hold complexity, learn through experiments and mobilize actors across the ecosystem. Obviously, being a pathfinder requires substantial leadership skills.

This is not a management theory book, and we approach leadership in a somewhat untraditional way. Here, we lean on the work of Frederic Laloux (2014) and Brian J. Robertson (2016), who have provoked conventional leadership thinking by introducing new organizational models that radically suggest we 'set people free' in organizations. Their latest models challenge leaders' influence, erasing hierarchy and bureaucracy to cultivate self-management, a sense of purpose, peer relationships, transparency and trust.

Inspired by this thinking, we stress that the leader is not one specific person who holds power over others, but that leadership is a skill set and way of being in the world that can be taken on by all kinds of people across society. Thus, the book acknowledges that all individuals, independent of their organizational context, can lead and become leaders.

The pathfinder is a leading role. We aim to increase agency among pathfinders, whether they hold a formal mandate or not, to lead societal change processes forward by obtaining clarity on how they might contribute most.

The leadership role in societal transition processes is often that of a convener and mobilizer of ways to collaborate across diverse groups of people. The role is notably *relational*, where decisions are shaped through relationships and networks rather than hierarchical structures.

This relational approach to leadership roles can gain inspiration from Actor Network Theory (ANT) pioneered by sociologist Bruno Latour (2007). ANT views social phenomena as the result of interactions within a network of actors, both human and non-human. Seen from a leadership perspective it accentuates how leaders emerge through their ability to connect and mobilize diverse actors. Agency is distributed among all actors in a network and therefore leadership can arise out of various corners in society, highlighting the *distributed* nature of influence. ANT stresses the importance of *translation* in building networks and mobilization. Learning from this way of thinking, we see leaders as people who take upon them the role of translation, negotiation and alignment so actors converge towards a common goal.

Continuing this distributed, convening and mobilizing role of the leader, we highlight the importance of building *followership* among people. We attach leadership capabilities to people who can induce followership towards a common direction. Leadership thinkers such as Simon Sinek (2019), Daniel Pink (2018) and Brené Brown (2018) advocate for leaders to do so by leading with and for purpose, building psychological safety, applying empathy, focusing on human connection and actively engaging people to give them autonomy, mastery and purpose.

Accordingly, sometimes the act of pathfinding demands us to step back and follow others – exercising followership. Here, pathfinders must pass on the mandate and support the brave individuals or groups who step forward and take action.

As we showcase throughout the book, leadership is not about mastering and obtaining specific power but about *navigating* with drive, empathy, humility and persistence.

Navigating a new story

Close your eyes. Imagine the future. What do you see?

You will probably have a relatively simple and recognizable image on your retina. Like many of us. Maybe you envision a society roughly like the one we know today but permeated with advanced technology, where the boundaries between humans and tech are blurry, and robots and artificial intelligence services interact as a naturally integrated part of your everyday routines. Or perhaps you envision an apocalyptic world on the verge of collapse? Where everything is chaotic and structures, as we know them, transportation, schools and nursing homes, are all falling apart?

During our many years of working with futures design while proactively developing, exploring and uncovering alternative versions of the future, we have asked hundreds of people this very question. The answers often fall into those two extremes: the same society with more advanced technology or a society that has fallen apart.

Only on very rare occasions do the answers paint a picture of positive alternatives to the society we live in today. It seems that we simply fail to imagine that life can be different from what we already know. That things could be better, life could be bigger, have more value and even a different meaning.

If this is the case, our limitations as to how we address the future have a tremendous impact on our ability to build new pathways out of the crises. We lack tangible images of a different future, and in turn, the opportunity space in which we look for new answers becomes too defined and too narrow. Our incentive to change things disintegrates.

It leaves us with a feeling of an increasingly missing ingredient: The ability to imagine a different tomorrow. Do we, as individuals and as a society, have the muscles, the capacity and the infrastructure to do so?

This navigation point focuses on the power of imagination and how we can shape new narratives to create a shared direction. Storytelling, immersive experiences and futures design hold an immense power in creating a collective sense of purpose across diverse groups of people, organizations, positions and agendas. It enables us to develop enticing, relatable and hopeful narratives about the future that can create a sense of directionality, commonality and longing for us in our endeavour to change society for the better. We hope this navigation point can give you the appetite and provide examples to concretize how to approach it.

We will take you through the following:

- Why we need to strengthen and train our ability to imagine.
- Which means and approaches we may apply to expand our outlook.
- How systems thinking can inform the narratives we create.
- Why we need to explore multiple alternative futures.
- How to collectively build a shared direction and a new story to mobilize people towards a preferred future.

2

The imagination crisis

Why is it so hard to imagine a better future? And, more importantly, what are the consequences if we fail?

According to Professor Geoff Mulgan, we struggle to imagine futures because 'future imagination involves two distinct steps, each of which is difficult: The first step involves questioning or rejecting the present, resisting to claim to be natural. The second step means constructing a plausible alternative, moving between an awareness of limits and a search for transcendence of those same limits' (Mulgan, 2022: 35).

It is no exaggeration to say that both of us, on several occasions, felt naive, on the verge of unintelligent, in the many situations where we have presented the idea about a sustainable and better future. Daring to imagine a better world. We have repeatedly encountered resistance or scepticism from others, which, honestly, at times, have made us doubt our own worldview.

This feeling is not unique to us. One of us, Julie, once reached out to her network on LinkedIn to invite people to give their version of how an irresistible, circular society might look and feel 30 years from now. She got this private response in her direct inbox from a business leader within concrete production:

> It is interesting that it is actually uncomfortable and daunting to respond to your question, Julie; hence, I reply through a private message. For me, it is a challenge to think of such large changes, imagining a life with the consumption level of the 1930s and

the technology of 2053. It seems absurd and almost silly. But on the other hand, as Einstein said: 'Doing the same thing over and over again and expecting a different result is the definition of insanity.'

After that, he moved on to answer the question. He described a moving image of himself as an 85-year-old cycling in 2053.

In a world wrapped tightly in fast-paced breaking news, rewarding short-term results and providing constant feedback from social media, long-term thinking and dreaming become scarce resources. Dreaming and visioning are profound ways to develop and operate our society, but they are not recognized and accepted. The grand and hopeful narrative is missing, as well as the small fragments of hopeful stories. The negative here-and-now stories dominate our public debate.

Should we care?

Our essential ability to imagine is quite central for us humans to be able to thrive (Heshmat, 2022). Studies that follow people who fall outside the labour market for a longer period find that these people gradually lose the ability to believe that their everyday life, both short-term and long-term, can be different and that they can be employed and have a work-life (DDC and Kolding Municipality, 2023). Young people who are unhappy and experience severe anxiety and school refusal are unable to imagine that their everyday life could be different – with school, friends and free time. 'Why are we failing at something that comes so naturally to us as children? Could it be that at this most critical point in our planet's history, when all our resources and senses are required, that we are not well equipped at all?' (Hopkins, 2019).

As we grapple with imagining positive alternatives to the pillars on which we have built our society – asking ourselves what our care and educational systems, welfare, workplaces, democracy or communities might look like in 30–40 years – it seems we have become less capable of doing so compared to the past (Mulgan, 2020). Our ability to reimagine new structures, logics and discourses is faltering.

In Mulgan's influential book on imagination, *Another World is Possible*, he points to studies showing 'that young people no longer expect to be better off than their parents, and that a pervasive pessimism has taken hold, whatever concerns democracy or the planet' (Mulgan, 2020: 14).

The devastating numbers from an international study published in 2021 echo that tendency: Two-thirds of young people aged 16–24 are feeling sad, afraid and anxious. Over half (56 per cent) say they think humanity is doomed (Harrabin, 2021). Up to 70 per cent feel scared or bleak when they think about the future and climate change. And one out of four women between the ages of 20 and 30 consider parenting to be out of reach, postponed or not desirable (Sandborg, 2023).

In Denmark, a study conducted by the National Danish Broadcasting Corporation showed that one in five Danes actively opts out of reading the news because they feel sad about the many negative stories, which shows an alarming sign of not only pessimism but resignation (Danmarks Radio, 2023).

The numbers speak for themselves. There seems to be an alarming connection between the rising crisis, the current state of mind and our decreasing ability to imagine.

Lacking incentives and structures

> We're too busy working on the ship, with no time to look for icebergs. (Polchar, 2021)

Like moths to a porch light on a summer night, we cannot help but gravitate towards technological solutions, even when they might not serve us best. For many years, we have been tied into a tenacious narrative that technology will save us. We just need to speed up our inventions, their adaptation and large-scale implementation. This technocratic vision holds a dangerous and wrong conclusion.

Can technology save us from chaos and give us the answer to our complex challenges? No. It will have a tremendous and vital role to play in society. But in our opinion, we need to move beyond the mindset of solving problems through engineering. There is a risk that a uniform view of technology as an almost divine power, unfortunately, becomes a pretext for inaction and complacency. Focusing solely on technological possibilities means we neglect the future generations, failing to consider how our decisions might affect their lives, emotions, and experiences.

In our view, many of society's current structures do not support or reward the use of imagination, and we do not train it as a skill or utilize the natural ability we all inherently have as children. In today's educational system, children are still taught traditional skills in a hierarchical order: put roughly, we attach importance to the natural sciences, subsequently, the social sciences and, at the bottom, the creative disciplines. Creativity and imagination are not only important for our ability to develop and innovate here and now. These skills are essential for tackling future challenges, developing and affecting societal progress, questioning the status quo, and developing alternative solutions. Hence, creativity is closely related to our ability to think critically and ask the questions that can propel our society forward. Creative thinking serves as a precondition for a strong and vibrant democracy.

Rob Hopkins, a transition pioneer and independent environmentalist, stresses that we must perceive imagination as something far more essential to our society:

> We have come to see imagination as a luxury. We need to move to see that it is absolutely not and that it should be fundamental to how our policy – and other aspects of public and private life – works. We need to create an environment where our imagination enshrines us. It needs to run through everything we do. (Hopkins, 2019)

According to Hopkins: 'We're suffering from pre-traumatic stress disorder – a constant background state of anxiety. When we have anxiety, the hippocampus shrinks by 20 percent, and we lose the ability to think about the future' (Hopkins, 2019).

If our space of opportunity is narrowed, then how do we train or rehabilitate our ability to imagine positive and alternative futures that we can aspire to? How do we recognize what we cannot see today?

How might we rediscover and reignite hope and belief of a better tomorrow by showing new pathways, also for the sake of coming generations' courage and leverage?

Our position is that we should care about our ability to imagine collectively and individually. That we need to be more concerned and preoccupied with how we train, develop and strengthen our imagination. It is important to strengthen and invest in the innovative and imaginative power of public organizations, non-governmental organizations, companies and citizens and constitute a more nuanced understanding and, not least a more proactive, intentional and conscious orientation towards the future.

The future seems unknown yet predictable

Try to envisage yourself on an aeroplane. The plane is on autopilot, the navigation system is switched on, and even though the aeroplane shakes due to heavy turbulence, there is nothing you can do.

Living in the 21st century, many of us have grown accustomed to the fact that our society and lives are affected by a growing change and increasing uncertainty and ambiguity. The gravity of the situation was underpinned when the COVID-19 crisis spread like wildfire in 2020–2021 because so did the tremendous consequences; much of what we took for granted changed overnight. And not just on a geopolitical level. It shook our very perception of what it means to be human. Of what it means to be together, both as families and friends. It affected our work, our schools, our nurseries, our hobbies, and even our habits around sharing a meal.

However, there have also been several other crises in recent times that have affected us widely and had extensive consequences on the way we live our lives. The financial crisis in 2008 led to significant restructuring in the public sector in several countries; the refugee crisis changed many countries' approaches to immigration and integration; the beginning of the war in Ukraine led to skyrocketing prices on convenience goods, electricity and gas and, thus, interest rates and mortgage payments. Recently, the escalation of the Israeli and Palestinian conflict has led to reinforced local war as well as a global political and cultural division between communities. These days, after the 2024 presidential election in the United States, we are witnessing political absurdity and unsettling escalation of geopolitical instability. As an alarming backdrop to all of this, the climate crisis, with recurrent wildfires, massive drought and extreme weather conditions, intensifies as a looming global threat to our very existence.

This ephemeral nature of our surroundings can leave us with the sense of a future that seems ambiguous, unknown and highly uncertain. Everything may change tomorrow, so our actions today may be meaningless.

To add further nuance, throughout our years of working with societal transitions with so many different people, an outspoken feeling of predetermination and powerlessness has been clearly present. Often, collaboration partners describe how they think past decisions and present actions have already been decided and that we are just passengers on a locked-in route. They feel a loss of control.

Growing fatalism and lack of hope in a future that can be different consequently result in a crumbling belief in our ability to affect our future. It seems simply not within our power to influence it.

But what is the truth about the future? For sure, it is not a fixed singular entity. It is a fluid, multiple, dynamic, moving set of outcomes and something we *can* affect. It does not just happen to you. It is, after all, affected by the actions we take and the decisions we make today. But how do we mobilize this motivation and re-inject agency?

In the recognition that the social challenges we face are complex, connected and dependent in many areas, the brutal truth that we do not know all the answers anymore gradually reveals itself to us. What is even more anxiety-provoking is that our known frameworks and methodologies that usually help us analyse and plan our way forward do not work anymore.

We cannot solve tomorrow's and certainly not the future's challenges with yesterday's solutions and methods. We need radical new thinking.

At the last national election in Denmark in 2022, several politicians openly and honestly acknowledged that they did not have the answers to several societal problems and that we must look for entirely new solutions when touching upon challenges such as the growing mental health crisis among young people, the ageing population and the decrease in healthcare professionals, just to mention a few.

A growing appetite

During the last four or five years of our careers, we have experienced a ripening in our collaborations: The recognition of wicked problems and systemic challenges has increased. Fortunately, the appetite for new approaches has grown along with it.

Wicked problems is a term gaining ground in recent years, not only in our Danish or Scandinavian collaborations but also in international partnerships and collaborations. The concept especially resonates within public sector innovation. *Wicked problems* are complex, coherent and dynamic, spanning institutions, administrations and systemic frameworks. The theory of wicked problems was first put forward by Rittel and Webber in 1973 in the context of social policy development (Rittel and Webber, 1973).

One reason why so much energy is being put into understanding and revitalizing the notion of wicked problems today is linked with the increasing realization in society that we remain unsuccessful in solving many of our problems. Several wicked problems are not new: they could, for instance, be about the persistently large number of people who remain outside the labour market and on the fringes of society or our lack of action in slowing down global warming. It is not like we have not tried. A substantial number of resources, time and energy have already been invested to try to fix these problems. Winhall and Leadbeater give wicked problems the incisive characteristics of being 'deeply rooted' as they seem to produce 'a persistent pattern of failure' (Leadbeater and Winhall, 2020). The *wickedness* calls on us to understand the problems differently and to approach them in a new way.

Table 2.1 illustrates the distinction between what we call tame problems and wicked problems, which can be helpful to distinguish between before venturing into the endeavour to try and tackle them.

Table 2.1: Tame problems versus wicked problems

Tame problems	Wicked problems
Relevant social, technological, economic, environmental and political factors are, to some degree, stable	Relevant social, technological, economic, environmental and political factors are unstable
Uncertainty is limited	Uncertainty is high
We are able to project the present into the future	We must imagine and consider multiple possible futures
The problem can be solved with known approaches	The problem needs reframing and requires new approaches
The ability to identify and develop the best solutions within the existing system is essential	The ability to navigate complexity and imagine alternative systems and opportunity spaces is essential
Possible to solve	Impossible to solve once and for all
Analysis is crucial	Imagination is crucial

As the concept has gained traction in recent years, there are also further developments and nuances that are worth considering.

In his Danish book on systemic issues, author and thinker Sigge Winther Nielsen criticizes Rittel and Webber by describing the notion of 'wicked problems' as overly pessimistic and 'malicious' (Winther Nielsen, 2023). As the term *wicked problems* suggests something unapproachable and unsolvable, it may deter many stakeholders from even attempting to confront them. Therefore, he introduces a new term in Danish, which can be freely translated into *wild problems*.

He defines wild problems as: 'Problems where there is varying degrees of consensus on the problem's definition, as well as varying degrees of consensus on possible solutions' (Winther Nielsen, 2023: 18). We are inclined to support his concern and appreciate this elaboration. Moving forward in the book, we use this as a backdrop for our referral to wicked problems.

A basic premise for addressing and influencing wicked problems is that we can only use the toolbox we usually use, for example, in public innovation, to a limited extent. Working with wicked problems entails maintaining complexity, which is critical as these problems are 'dynamic and, in principle, impossible to solve because the challenges they describe are constantly moving. When we interact with the problem, it changes. New connections and entanglements arise. New resource flows appear. The appearance of the problem changes' (Østergaard et al, 2023: 1).

Even if new complementary or alternative systems overcome the structural conditions that have created dysfunctional situations today, it would still be utopian to imagine that they would be flawless and able to solve such large-scale problems completely. The problem will continue to change its form, and the understanding of it will grow and become more nuanced. Naturally, as a result, ambitions and goals will evolve, too. Therefore, it is not meaningful to talk about the final solutions to wicked problems but rather, to instigate, accelerate and guide the system in a better direction.

Changing the systems

> Institutions that were designed for one set of problems in another era are now being tasked to come up with solutions to quite different challenges in a different context. (Leadbeater and Winhall, 2020)

The wicked problems highlight paradoxes in both our social and societal construction and articulate the necessity of fundamentally changing the way our systems are designed and operate if we are to succeed in creating long-term and sustainable impacts for people, society and, ultimately, our planet. It is not an easy task to change systems. In her research, Engholm describes a system as something that is self-sustaining and self-organizing. Therefore, the system will always push back when we try to implement change (Engholm, 2023). We, thus, need other ways to unlock these structures.

As Leadbeater and Winhall propose, '[s]ystemic challenges are characterised by a structural mismatch between institutions, the context they work in and the needs they meet. A systemic challenge reveals fundamental issues about the purpose of a system and how it is organised to serve society' (Leadbeater and Winhall, 2020). Meaning that, in order to address and influence wicked problems, we need to start investigating why systems work the way they do, and design and support the emergence of new and more sustainable complementary systems that, over time, even eclipse the existing system.

The book *Thinking in Systems* from 2008 compiles and publishes Donella Meadows' three decades of work with systems thinking. In her work, Meadows emphasizes the impact systems thinking offers: a different way of seeing the world and understanding the parts of a system and the whole simultaneously, which is crucial for addressing complex problems like inequality, the refugee crisis, loneliness, the demographic imbalance – ageing population and decrease in birth rate, to mention a few. Meadows stresses that systems thinking is essential for recognizing that problems often stem from the structure of the systems themselves.

Meadows points our attention to 'traps' in the system, for example, policy resistance and escalation, consequently when systems by themselves act counterproductively or even harmfully. Furthermore, she points to the fact that those system traps can be escaped and translated into opportunities for change: 'by recognising them [system traps] in advance and not getting caught in them, or by altering the structure – by reformulating goals, by weakening, strengthening, or altering feedback loops, by adding new feedback loops' (Meadows, 2008: 112). In that sense, one can argue, just as fellow systems thinkers from this decade do, that we need to understand structures, logics and behaviours in the system to recognize the leverage points for change.

Let us zoom in on Leadbeater and Winhall's excellent work with system innovation. The two system innovators provide us with a framework, 'the four keys', which allows us to investigate a problem from different vantage points, which, each in its own way, opens up a redefinition and even the designing of a new system. The four keys help us explore:

1. the purpose of a system;
2. how it affects the distribution of power;
3. which recognized and available resources the system consists of; and
4. which relationships affect and determine the system.

It enables us to point to new understandings, logics and discourses more easily.

In the following, we try to briefly summarize Leadbeater and Winhall's four keys, how they interact and, thus, can support us in unlocking systems (Leadbeater and Winhall, 2020):

- *Purpose.* According to Leadbeater and Winhall, the most powerful way to transform a system is by changing its purpose and the underlying philosophy that defines it. System innovators – in our case, the pathfinders – achieve this by creating solutions rooted in a new operating mindset that demonstrates a different system purpose. This new purpose becomes the organizing point for people, activities and resources, often requiring a reimagining of the system's goals. Such changes are driven by debates, creativity and visioning. Repurposing ties into storytelling and building new narratives.
- *Power.* It is nearly impossible to change a system's purpose without shifting the power balances. The notion of who holds the power to control resources, set priorities and define success. The power within systems is complex; it manifests itself in both hard and soft forms and is often deeply embedded in culture. System innovators, the pathfinders, challenge existing power structures, which can lead to disagreements and conflicts over priorities as new systems emerge. These power shifts are deeply tied to changes in the flow of resources and relationships within the system.
- *Resources.* A system undergoes significant change when the flow of resources within it is fundamentally altered. This can occur during crises, when traditional resources are constrained, forcing innovators to develop new methods to meet needs. Conversely, new systems can emerge when novel resources, like digital technologies, become available at low cost. Repurposing can also open new resources to flow. Resource flows in a system extend beyond money and technology. It also includes action, knowledge and reputation. When working to find new pathways, we seek to unlock and mobilize these resources to create better outcomes and discover new paths.
- *Relationships.* The system consists of a set of components that repeatedly come together to produce a result, forming an interconnected whole rather than isolated elements. These relationships, rather than the individual parts themselves, give

a system its character. This is particularly characteristic of social systems, where key relationships like purchaser and supplier, politicians and citizens, employer and employee, doctor and patient, or teacher and pupil are foundational. When a system faces challenges, tensions often rise within these relationships, leading to strain and dissatisfaction. Systemic change often involves creating new patterns of relationships, leading to new social models. Hence, pathfinders will not just extend existing models; they create solutions that reconfigure relationships, enabling new value creation. For example, new systems emerge when actors are brought together in new ways, when structures that are usually centralized become decentralized, or when consumers are transformed into active participants and equal co-producers.

The four keys in practice

We will turn to the Netherlands for a case that exemplifies how the four keys unlock new opportunities. In the early and mid-2010s, the Hestia project experimented with restructuring the power of the Dutch system of youth care. In the project, young people in foster care were given more autonomy and influence. Contrary to what is the norm in many countries' youth care systems, where the contact person is employed by the authorities, the project flipped the system: the contact person was selected by the young people themselves. The contact person received special training in relevant laws and regulations to ensure they could effectively represent the child's rights and best interests on equal terms. The goal of this initiative was to empower the youth and, hence, provide them with a support system they trusted. This project aligned with the broader reforms in Dutch youth care, emphasizing child participation and personalized care under their Youth Act (Project Hestia, 2018).

The results of the Dutch case underline the shift in power dynamics and the purpose: the young people have the power, and the system's purpose is to empower them and enable them to make the right decisions for *their* lives and to provide safety and trust. The young people gained more ownership over their own situation, better well-being and a sense of control. Their previously locked-in role as recipients of a public service dissolved. In addition, the shift not only introduced entirely new resources into the system but also gave relationships new significance.

The four keys help us gain a deeper understanding of the embedded structures, values and norms within systems and the logics and array of acceptable solutions. They provide us with a better understanding of the lock-ins and where we need to turn the keys to unlock new opportunities.

As we explore how to build new narratives that inspire and mobilize the transgressing of our existing systems, it is helpful to keep in mind how narratives and storytelling can depict new purposes, power structures, resources and relationships that challenge and provoke our conventional thinking. Thus, the four keys give us a set of tools which can open up a conversation that is richer, more explorative, curious and more imaginative.

In that sense, system innovation is closely connected with futures design and can mutually enrich each other. When we explore multiple, diverse alternative futures, we push the boundaries of what we can imagine. This can open our eyes to entirely new possibilities and risks. When we give life to alternative realities, the logic of our system becomes more apparent. Invisible mechanisms, power relations and relationships that we never imagined could be different, suddenly become visible and may even seem obtainable. Without this awareness, we risk building systems that look new on the surface but reproduce existing problems underneath.

Later, we will unfold and dive deeper into the four keys and how the reframing of the system around *mental health* and *well-being* created a set of new opportunities.

An era of opportunities?

Now that we have touched upon the status quo regarding the seriousness of the wicked problems we face, including our collective lack of imagination, let us zoom out for a second to take a more optimistic angle on our society's preconditions for developing an alternative outcome of the future.

It is a paradox that while the challenges and crises pile up and the world seems to become more turbulent than ever before, we also have the most skilled workforce in history, and we see the emergence of new and more effective ways of organizing ourselves. Technological innovation indeed gives us new opportunities for reframing challenges, and COVID-19 provided us with a clear example of how fast we can change habits and behaviours.

The world has never been more closely connected than it is today. Thanks to the internet, social media and other digital technologies, we can communicate seamlessly across the globe. We trade across many borders and exchange products, ideas, knowledge and, yes, culture. Today, we create deep connections and vital life relationships through digital tools. Could that physical and digital connectedness hold enormous potential if we shift our focus?

Igniting hope and agency

If we look closely, a current is moving, seemingly growing stronger. It signifies a paradigm shift of critical voices that challenge today's current capitalistic structures and logics in the wake of increasing anxiety and with the transgression of planetary boundaries. This new current invites an exciting systemic repurposing as people around the world explore how it might manifest. More are gathering around it, and it has momentum. It gives us hope, as it can support and accelerate pathfinders in erasing some of the structures and patterns that are so entrenched in systems today.

According to Engholm, the Western world has been caught up in disruption and production loops ever since the Great Acceleration, making and rethinking without reflecting on learning from past experiences or considering where we want to go and what expected outcomes we need for our future. Engholm states, 'In the beginning, we designed products to fulfil our needs. Now, we design new needs that satisfy our products' (Engholm, 2023: 151).

We are tempted to ask whether today's designers, developers, policy makers and engineers dare to ask themselves the obvious question: am I solving a problem or creating a new need?

Whether or not Engholm depicts a lasting trend, we can only speculate, but fortunately, we do see cracks in this tendency, especially among younger activists whose voices are getting louder.

Perhaps we have become so used to our society being driven by monetary profit and prosperity that we have completely missed that it could be otherwise? As Fredric Jameson puts it: 'Someone once said that it is easier to imagine the end of the world than to imagine the end of capitalism' (Jameson, 2003: 76).

We recognize these ideas and the critique of the existing economic paradigm in the memo *On the Emergence of the Ecological Class*, written by Nikolaj Schultz and the late Bruno Latour in 2022. With this publication, the two sociologists explore whether it is possible to create an ideology around ecology that is equally powerful to socialism and liberalism. With the idea of an emerging ecological class they suggest that traditional class structures based on economic factors (working class, middle class, upper class) are becoming increasingly irrelevant in the face of the global ecological crisis. The new *ecological class* is defined by its relationship to the environment, its environmental awareness and its willingness to act on climate change:

> Our mental, moral, organisational, administrative, and legal frameworks, which have been associated with development for so long, are now idling because they were designed to focus on what is now a dead end [increased productivity]. Today, it's clear that the direction of things has changed, but the new tools that would enable us to take action have not yet been developed. We're stuck in anxiety, guilt, and powerlessness. It is the role of the ecological class to provide these tools. (Latour and Schultz, 2022: 27)

In an interview, Schultz point to some of the levers that he suggests can be applied to ignite political agency and mobilize political action towards ecology. 'The problem with ecology has been the assumption that we would act once we knew the extent of the catastrophe', says Schultz.

> Either out of a deterministic idea that we must act in order to survive, or out of a moral obligation that we should. But we need the will to act, and that necessary cultural change can happen, among other things,

through art: short stories, songs, films, visual art. ... There have been countless pop songs about freedom, individuality, and love, but none about climate change. (Kongstad, 2024)

This lack of ability to think beyond our existing economic structures is something we personally recognize from our work with sustainable transition. In our efforts to advance the transition to a circular economy, we have met and engaged with several people who stumble to formulate a positive narrative regarding a sustainable future. We have experienced how the dominant narrative around climate change is that of restrictions and constraints and even, to some, a reduction of freedom.

The majority of literature, news and public conversations regarding climate change are marked with the underlying pessimism of the dark consequences of human progress and a personal and collective shame about the effects of human actions – our incessant flying, shopping and devouring of red beef steaks. We struggle to imagine something different or better that is in clear contrast to where human progress has brought us today. 'Science has very clearly told us what we need to leave behind, but we don't really know what we're moving towards. What might it look like? How might it smell? What might it sound like?' says Ditte Lysgaard Vind (2024), a Danish expert on design and circular transition.

In the context of creating sustainable futures, Rob Hopkins' work on the concept of longing offers an interesting nuance regarding our imagination crisis and the stories we tell, highlighting the need to build new narratives. He suggests that what we are truly lacking is a sense of longing or desire for a different future. Hopkins emphasizes that without a deep desire or longing for change, our imaginative capacities diminish, and we lose the ability to envision alternative futures. His work, like Latour's and Schultz's, encourages practices that nurture this creative capacity, such as storytelling, scenario planning and engaging with the arts, all of which help translate abstract desires into tangible pathways for the future (Hopkins, 2020).

Following this, we argue that when we collaboratively create a new narrative that paints a different future, it provides us with images and experiences that are distinct and compelling. Through the tangible and sensory, we rediscover the world. In doing so, we cultivate this longing for something different, something we have already felt. And this inspires action.

Well-being economy: a profound way of repurposing the system

Considering several researchers' criticism of our existing economic model and various attempts to generate new perspectives and ideas, it is worth taking a closer look at the emergence of a new narrative on our economy that may potentially contribute to a profound shift in how we understand and design our systems today: the well-being economy.

The well-being economy has been introduced as a new and unifying framework for a joint dialogue around our connected crises. It is designed deliberately to work for people and the planet, not the other way around. In a well-being economy, the rules, norms and incentives that shape the economy are set up to encourage activities that deliver quality of life and flourish for all people, in harmony with our environment, by default (Trebeck and Smith, 2024). Well-being economists argue that in spite of several years of stable economic growth, our societies are in the midst of both an environmental and social decline as we today transgress six out of nine planetary boundaries and, at the same time, witness a steady decline in mental well-being.

The new way of thinking is a break with the narrow focus on economic growth as the default purpose of many of our societal systems. It reorientates political and economic decision making towards more far-reaching, sustainable goals instead of a shortsighted hunt for profits. It acknowledges the economic system as an important means to drive resources, but challenges the fact that growth and gross domestic product are the ultimate goals. Furthermore, well-being economists work to provide decision-making guides, frameworks, economic models and sound data for politicians to analyse, document and argue for the broad and multidimensional interpretation of well-being.

In our view, the well-being economy is especially powerful because it, as Schultz and Latour argue, places aspirational ideas of well-being as a new purpose. Instead of arguing towards the negation of growth, it gives a competing and compelling new purpose rather than locking us down in a polarised debate on growth versus degrowth.

In her newest book, *Underskud* [*Deficit*], the Danish feminist and debater Emma Holten opens with a provocative reference to a study that states how women are unprofitable for the economy: Women – in economic terms – are costs: We take more money out of the national economy than we give back, due to childbirth and our time spent on maternity leave. Furthermore, there are numerous invisible care tasks that women are often expected to undertake, such as managing children's sick days and caring for elderly relatives. Holten makes the argument to challenge the way we calculate the value of work in public policy, highlighting the obvious flaws in how society fails to calculate the relational and social value of work (Holten, 2024).

It is inspiring to follow the evolution of a different economic paradigm, as it provides new and refreshing perspectives on existing structures and logics that are deeply embedded in our lives, by providing sound arguments for a more holistic and sustainable approach to organizing society. In our view, the well-being economy repurposes our systems and provides us with both a tool and a legitimacy to reconfigure them. When we no longer place growth and gross domestic product at the centre and as the end goal of many of the things we do in our society, a range of new opportunities, solutions and initiatives emerge.

Expanding our perspective through futures design

We promote an exploration of the more ambiguous aspects of the future. More importantly, we argue for a multidimensional and empathetic perspective on the future if we are to act proactively on it in the present, be it as citizens, policy makers, technologists, entrepreneurs or business leaders. To do so, we need different means. We need to expand our outlook. And perhaps it is not so much about looking for the icebergs, as Polchar states earlier in this section, but for fairways through the ice floes and icebergs.

Imagination is not a gift but a skill that can be trained by all people. Fortunately, there are several ways to rehabilitate our imagination. The domain of *futures design*, encompassing disciplines such as strategic foresight, alternative futures and scenario development, speculative design and storytelling, can play a crucial and powerful role in aiding us towards the future. *Futures design* offers tools and approaches for working proactively with the future. It helps us train our imagination and provides us with concrete images of what alternative futures might look like. These alternative images of the future can help us shine a different light on the challenges we know today to uncover our blind spots, reframe our approaches to a problem and reveal possible pathways for moving towards something better. This, we argue, is a prerequisite for navigating a new story for societal change.

Let us dive into a concrete Danish case that illustrates how imagining alternative futures can shed a different light on one of the major current challenges we face as society today: a healthcare system on its knees.

Unlocking the system of healthcare

In Denmark, our life expectancy is longer than ever. As the population grows older, we increasingly live with multiple chronic conditions that would have been deadly in the recent past. We experience treatments getting better and more specialized. Naturally, our expectations of the healthcare system are changing as well – and rightfully so.

Despite the progress, however, we see a growing gap between the services and experiences we expect as citizens and patients and what the current system is able – and in some cases willing – to offer. On top of this, there is the fast-growing challenge of educating enough healthcare professionals to care for the increasing ageing population, if we continue to organize and deliver healthcare as we do today. This growing demand places immense pressure on healthcare systems, exacerbating existing workforce shortages (World Health Organization, 2016). In addition, we see public budget cutbacks and, consequently, rising inequality. The challenge is wicked and systemic: intertwined, multifaceted and complex. The problem is well-known at all stages in society: Recent elections in 2022 showed health and hospitals to be the most important topic for Danes when casting their votes (Larsen and Hansen, 2022).

Here is a clear example of our imagination crisis: despite the obvious need for rethinking the healthcare system entirely, we have a really hard time imagining the future of health beyond simply new technologies or treatments. Our vision for the future of healthcare is unclear and entangled with challenging ideological logics and ethical questions locked in today's interpretation. This is to a point where we imagine the future healthcare as synonymous to technology, which essentially means hospitals of today with the medicine and technology of tomorrow.

'It takes several years to train and qualify as a gastroenterologist. But are we training them for the future or yesterday's medicine? Are we fighting yesterday's war?' asks Rafael Ramirez in his course on scenario planning at Oxford University and Saïd Business School in 2020.

What if the purpose of our healthcare system was to enable citizens to live meaningful, healthy lives – instead of lives without diseases and symptoms? Would it promote well-being, prevention and the enhancement of life quality, and outshine the existing system's approach to addressing disease and treatment?

To be fair, we must mention that over the last three years, we have seen weak signals and local signs of the healthcare sector beginning to explore, experiment and ask radical new questions, such as how healthcare could be experienced, organized, provided, administered, regulated and, not least, valued. During a panel debate one of us contributed in, Sara, a representative from an industry association, notably said from the stage to the audience: 'Companies must not only be able to deliver on efficiency; they must deliver more value for patients and employees. Value is multifaceted and complex – we must not forget this in the work of developing the life science industry' (Tech BBQ, 2024).

To follow that train of thought, consider this: a hospital ward being measured on well-being and how many times a long-term admitted patient goes out to the garden during their stay, instead of the flow and numbers of patients fully treated and discharged. That would entail a whole new system, workflow and view on value creation and distribution of resources.

Alternative futures for the Danish healthcare system: Boxing Future Health

With this offset and motivation, let us have a look at a healthcare case from the Danish Design Center, carried out as a design process utilizing futures design to analyse changes that may occur in the future, as well as to inform the decisions made in the present.

Boxing Future Health was co-created with 100+ experts and professionals with backgrounds ranging from technology experts to doctors, priests, designers and scientists – mainly from the Danish ecosystem. The result of the co-creation process was four distinct visions of health in the year 2050.

These four alternative future scenarios were organized in a 2x2 matrix around two key dimensions: *the notion of health* and *the organization of healthcare*, as illustrated and elaborated in Figure 2.1.

The notion of health and disease: body versus life

The notion of health and disease and our body and life and how the body interacts with its surroundings.

- Body: The notion of health and disease is related to the body as the dominant perspective in the biomedical paradigm, which prevails in large parts of the healthcare sector around the world. It is rooted in a long-standing tradition that has led to many medical advances and to the structures framing our current healthcare system.
- Life: The alternative notion views the body as intertwined with life as it unfolds in a cultural and social context, framed by a different interpretation perspective – a perspective that goes beyond the body and places a significant emphasis on psychological, social and personal aspects as well as philosophical and the spiritual.

The organization of healthcare: collective versus individual

The organization and structures of future healthcare, spanning from a collective healthcare system to an individually oriented and multifaceted system:

- Collective: The collective healthcare system offers universal healthcare and legally mandated easy and equal access to healthcare services. The system is predominantly tax-based and provided by a public healthcare sector.

Figure 2.1: Boxing Future Health matrix

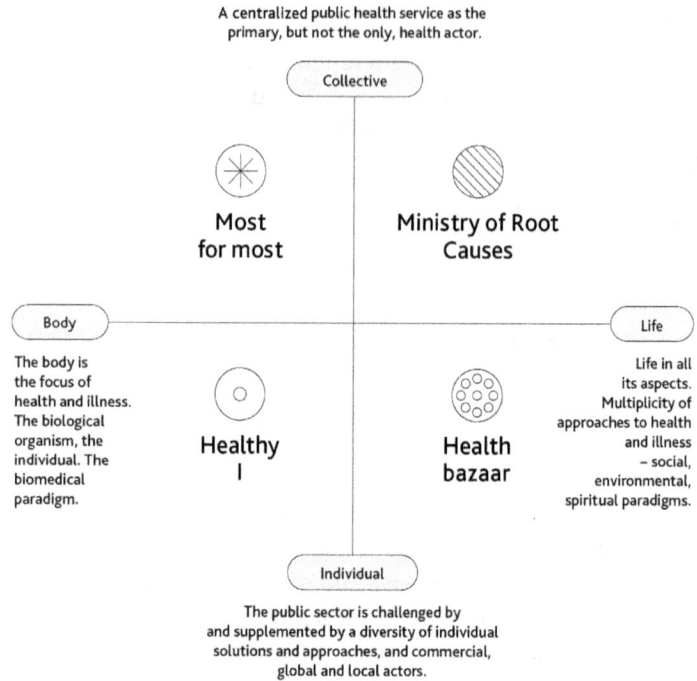

Source: DDC (2018a)

- Individual: The 'individual' organization of healthcare refers to a more individualized healthcare, where the patient and healthcare consumer has a much wider claim to individual healthcare services. A large and varied field of actors provide many different approaches and payment models. This is a more diverse and composite healthcare system (DDC, 2018b).

The four future scenarios

Within the intersections of these two dimensions, four plausible and distinct futures scenarios emerged. These are discussed in the following subsections.

Most for most

The healthcare sector is a core public welfare service. The emphasis is on broad issues and solutions. Improved life expectancy, widespread diseases and equal access to healthcare services are important goals, and most patients, who after all suffer from the most common diseases, receive good treatment. However, the National Board of Health makes tough priorities, and Denmark cannot keep its leading position when it comes to cutting-edge treatment options and healthcare technologies.

Healthy I

Technology and new business models generate new and intense dynamics in the healthcare sector and shift the boundaries of health and disease. People are keenly engaged in their own personal health and take advantage of the many new options for prevention, diagnosis, treatment and performance enhancement. The public healthcare sector is striving to adapt and take advantage of new opportunities, yet its function largely resembles that of a public utility.

Ministry of Root Causes

The Ministry of Root Causes sits at the head of the table when policy decisions are made, also in the broader political priorities, as once known from the role of the Ministry of Finance. The objective is to eliminate the root causes of disease and to promote sources of health. The focus is on providing good, healthy basic living conditions – a healthy society. This includes a holistic view on environment, working life, traffic, food production, lifestyle habits and personal relationships. Health concerns are an integrated aspect across all policy areas and a key driver of societal development. 'Make life fit' is the current slogan in the Ministry of Root Causes.

Health bazaar

Health is more than the body and the absence of disease. It is about life itself and a search for meaning. The narrow and rigid view on diseases characterizing the traditional biomedical paradigm is increasingly challenged. The result is not a new uniform paradigm but rather a noisy bazaar of divergent and mutually competing approaches and beliefs.

Welcome to the health bazaar. The bazaar has many different perceptions of health. It has booths, vendors, buyers. There are debates. There are stages. You're on stage. You're an expert. You are searching.

Health used to be so simple. It was the doctor's exclusive domain, and the doctor focused on the body. On mechanics. It was simple, but it felt reassuring. The biomedical paradigm. The biomedical paradigm was successful for a long time. Like the church. Once, it was practically the only thing people believed in. But it offers no understanding of life. And it has no right to define it. It has no right to reject other, broader understandings.

What sort of science do you believe in?

Which path is the right one for you? For your children? For our society?

'IS THERE A DOCTOR PRESENT ... Traffic's crazy. Pure chaos. The worst ones are the people who insist on driving their own cars. Smack! Busted board and a broken leg. Got a ride to the ER, though. That's when the fun begins. Lengthy explanations about the hospital's treatment approach and their concept of health and illness. I mean, a broken leg, how hard can it be, right?! Then the doctor comes in and wants to know how I feel about X-rays and electromagnetic radiation. Do I take neo morphine? Have I been bio-hacked? Do I belong to any particular health community? And so on and so forth. And lengthy explanations about what she thinks and what she stands for. I'm thinking, can't we just get this over with and move on? Then there's all the documentation. Stop! Just slap some plaster on, please. I know, that was in the old days, and we're so much wiser now, but ... IS THERE A DOCTOR PRESENT WITH SOME PLASTER?'

(DDC, 2018c)

You just read Elisabeth's story. She is 42 years old in 2050. She has a broken leg and shares a glimpse of her life in one of the four scenarios, the health bazaar, which gives us an impression of what a different future could look like and what it would feel like to actually take part in.

Immersing into alternative futures

Boxing Future Health as a future resource attempts to push the discussion beyond the notion of technology as the main lifeline, which forces us to focus on human aspects. The four scenarios were transformed into physical installations you could walk into, immerse yourself in and explore through audio narratives, just like Elisabeth's story. One would listen to the same three future citizens, Peter, Michael and Elisabeth, who live radically different lives in the four scenarios. Each scenario prompts their own answers to the question: What does it feel like to be human in 2050? How do we treat our bodies? What is illness? What does healthcare look like? And what do we even think of as 'health'?

The four scenarios were designed with an individual and distinct identity in terms of colour, iconography, atmosphere and feeling, with background audio, tactile elements and visuals. The participants were guided in smaller groups through each of the scenarios: Sometimes, they were blindfolded and had to explore with their hands; sometimes, they had to taste or smell; sometimes, they had to take off their shoes; and sometimes they had to lie down.

While the differences and characteristics of each scenario can be explained in detail through a report or presentation, it would require a great deal of both time and energy for the participants to develop a mutual understanding of them as well as the ability to distinguish between them. We found it much more effective to let people step into these futures and experience them on their own bodies through human stories. First, activating our senses and our empathy triggers a stronger emotional response faster and with a better retention rate. Second, because it is universal, it mitigates hierarchy and focuses on the human aspects that we can all relate to.

When a group of colleagues, with different titles and seniority, experience and physically immerse themselves in the four alternative futures together, they create a framework for discussing potentials and challenges from the same point of departure. With an outset in the same bodily experiences and audiological input of listening to people tell their stories and showing glimpses of their everyday lives, it became much easier for them to relate to them. Human to human. Mirroring themselves in each other. Building empathy. As such, the experience becomes a *boundary object*: A plastic piece of information that can be interpreted and used differently by different people while still being robust enough to be identified as being the same (Star and Griesemer, 1989).

As a dean from the University College Copenhagen put it after a longer strategy process facilitated through an exploration of the framework and scenarios:

> We have thought about some things we otherwise would not have thought about – and we have done that together. We have achieved a common understanding of what we are looking into and, thus, a shared frame of reference. This shared frame has brought us closer together across the management team. ... The process of working with the scenarios shows that you cannot simply look at one single profession at a time because when the healthcare system changes as it does, it has an impact on all professions. What a nurse does today, what medical laboratory technician does today, what a physiotherapist does today – maybe is not as clearly defined going forward. That has been an important realisation. (DDC, 2018d)

What is even more important, having a shared reference point in the far future instead of in the present makes it easier for people to open up and engage with the topic. Some of the delicate subjects get less emotional and difficult when they are framed decades beyond the next election. In this way, scenarios can help facilitate a constructive dialogue on otherwise, complex and daunting topics among diverse groups of people (Ramirez and Wilkinson, 2016).

Anchoring scenarios in the Danish healthcare sector

Boxing Future Health was initiated along with five close partners who all contributed with unique perspectives: two hospitals, two educational institutions and one industry association. The aim from the beginning and throughout the process was to ignite and inspire ambition and visionary direction for the future of health through dialogue in a way that was transferable for the partners to convert into action in their respective organizations.

But Boxing Future Health became much more than that. Besides being a useful open resource that works both in short-term development processes and long-term initiatives, the whole concept is adopted and integrated into the practice of one of the key partner organizations. University College Copenhagen implemented the core principles from the concept in a permanent setting. This means that all healthcare students at the University College are trained in alternative futures and multi-perspective thinking around healthcare, care and systems. Today, it builds capacity with the coming generations of healthcare professionals to continuously orient themselves towards the future and be adaptable. It provides them with a set of critical glasses to question the status quo and what the future might look like. This holds a huge, shared value in the health ecosystem in Denmark and its further development; not only when new professionals enter the labour market, but for many years to come. It prepares the ground for a common narrative about the future.

Since 2018 more than 6,000 people from across the healthcare sector, both public and private, international and national, ranging from executives to healthcare students, have used Boxing Future Health as a basis for dialogue and a trigger for change.

Reflections in a time of transition

In the spring of 2024, the Danish government received a set of recommendations (640 pages!) from an impartial group of high-level experts on how to restructure, reorganize and rethink healthcare in the small country of Denmark. It was the foundation for a reform of the Danish healthcare system.

Whether the commission, a group of respected and highly skilled professionals from the established system, had the ability to really rethink the structures and challenge their assumptions around healthcare, is difficult to determine. But we cannot help wondering: What if the commission included professionals from the design field or the arts? If their imagination was challenged to dream about a different future – what would their recommendations look like or feel like if they had the chance to really, deeply engage in alternative futures for healthcare?

At the time of writing, the recommendations have yet to be implemented in the forthcoming reform. Meanwhile, we will be waiting in anticipation.

3

A preferred future

It should be clear now that scenario design and futures design can open up and help us claim the opportunity spaces that wicked problems hold. Three or four diverse scenarios, however, do not provide a unified direction to work towards. Instead, they lay the rich and insightful groundwork for guiding a collective journey towards *the preferred future*.

One might be tempted to criticize that we focus on the wrong things if we focus or work towards preferred futures, thereby neglecting today's massive challenges and the many people already deeply affected by issues today like the effects of climate change. We turn to futures designer Oskar Stokholm Østergaard, whom we have collaborated with for many years, to nuance this:

> Others will argue that we desperately need the hope and radical ideas of preferred futures to escape the grip of the slowly collapsing status quo. I've found that working with both alternative and preferred futures in combination yields the best results for the transition-inspired work I am doing, especially when coupled with thorough backcasting, an attention to non-linear transition pathways, and a focus on immediate action and experimentation. (Østergaard, 2024a)

Through our experimentation with different corners of futures design, we have realized that driving processes that include a collective exploration of various plausible and possible and even extreme futures enable an essential next step: the convergence around a preferred future that nurtures collective understanding, urgency and hopefulness – and a very important ingredient: directionality.

Setting direction is about negotiating and choosing a direction – to give our intentions guidance. It is about committing to a goal and pursuing it, but also making choices, selections as well as deselections.

A shared direction – the preferred future – can mobilize actors across society, draw new lines and reveal interdependencies between stakeholders. It can create a sense of connectedness and belonging – even a feeling of collective vigour. A preferred future can become that trellis upon which our interventions in the present can grow (Østergaard et al, 2023).

The concept of the *preferred future* as a long-term guiding star for directionality can create enthusiasm and eagerness and a new opportunity for pathfinders and their collaborators to lean into. It becomes the new story that can be the guiding star you can repeatedly turn your eyes towards, as the campfire you gather around. In that sense, a preferred future becomes the direction that we can relate to, understand and dream of: What does this future look like? Which new opportunities arise? What lives can citizens live? What is the future for humanity, other species and for the planet? This accentuates the importance of the narrative.

As anthropologist David Graeber puts it beautifully simply: 'The ultimate, hidden truth of the world is that it is something that we make and could just as easily make differently' (Graeber, 2016: 89).

Do not underestimate your role as a pathfinder here. The connectivity the preferred future can create offers a language and a compelling narrative to latch onto. Circling back to the beginning of this book, acknowledging the need for new spaces to convene, remember this: You help by creating and holding an exploration space of opportunities for those who waver and doubt the existing system and its logic, those who sit quietly in meetings, or those who have realized that something else must be done, but do not know how to proceed.

It makes sense; a good story about a possible future where systems work differently, and the lives within them are better, can encapsulate and communicate the hope and nuance we so desperately need. Let us have a look at a concrete example, within one of the major societal challenges, *mental health for young people*.

Our city: Vorby

31 May 2023: The DDC, along with 150 partners and stakeholders from across the mental health landscape, invited decision makers and innovators on a journey through time to another world – a preferred future where young people thrive. The destination was the future city, Vorby (Bason and Striegler, 2023).

A city map was handed out, showing key historical landmarks, communal houses, institutions, cultural offerings and suggestions on where to start exploring. In Vorby, the participants had the chance to engage with local Vorby residents in discussions about learning, contributions to the community and leisure activities. Here, one could gain insight into and learn how the seven foundational principles that underpin the community shape the structures, the relations, the resources and the power in the city. For example, one principle of Vorby describes well-being as a shared responsibility rather than an individual one. The participants could also embark on an interactive tour to explore Vorby at their own pace.

'The imprint that the experience of being in the future has left on me will last. I will keep returning to these images in my daily work', one of the participants reflected after the time travel.

If we look to neuroscience, it indicates that we remember concrete experiences better than abstract knowledge, because the concrete appeals to several senses (Schilhab et al, 2008). The experience not only leaves its mark but even triggers action.

The city of Vorby is an image of the preferred future, created as a result of a comprehensive co-creation and scenario-driven process along with the many discussions, perspectives, dreams and decisions between the 150 people.

The journey to Vorby was the culmination of nearly a year of interdisciplinary and cross-sectoral in-depth and exploratory work, focused on exploring weak signals, plausible, possible and impossible scenarios to find a new shared direction, the preferred future. It was initiated in response to a complex and highly relevant development in societies worldwide: Young people's well-being in free fall. The Danish National Health Profile in 2021 confirmed the growing suspicion regarding declining mental health among young people in Denmark: one in three women and one in five men aged 16–24 experience anxiety, stress and loneliness.

The initiative was originally initiated in a partnership between a recognized Danish research fund and the Danish Design Center, combining research and analysis of mental health with a radical method to explore, challenge and develop the field. Despite numerous questions pointing in multiple directions and equally diverse ideas about the causes, the diagnosis was evident: as the established system reproduces the challenges, we need radically new approaches to grasp and address the problem.

A scaffold for new dialogues

Vorby provided a framework for a new type of dialogue and understanding without providing all the answers upfront. The answers were to be uncovered through conversations across individuals, organizations and silos. However, Vorby suggested repurposing our system with concrete images and a fictional reality to explore. Here, one could discover new relationships and resources that one previously did not have access to or were simply blind to. Using such a concrete and familiar cultural product as the city, we connected with the visitors and enabled them to form new connections. The city as a framework is inviting and inclusive, allowing many more people to contribute and engage.

As we argued in the case of Boxing Future Health, Vorby is another example of a boundary object that connects people into a shared human experience. In the anthology *Wild Problems*, edited by systems thinker Sigge Winther Nielsen, we described the resource Vorby possesses as a boundary object. 'Listening to actual – essentially fictional – people tell their stories, the complex problem becomes more accessible to relate to, regardless of one's skills and background. Therefore, even though actors may have different and even conflicting interests, we can foster a constructive dialogue' (Bason and Striegler, 2023: 206–207).

Using sound, images and stories from the citizens of Vorby made the future concrete, relatable and accessible. Every stakeholder in the process could interpret and analyse their organization's role in Vorby, the products and services, collaborations and skills they would need in this future city. By placing people with detailed characteristics and life conditions in different futures, we could mirror ourselves and, thus, spark empathy and connect with situations that could happen and be of considerable importance. The stories stuck with us. As researcher Cynthia Selin points out: 'Narratives stretch plausibility and create memorability' (Selin, 2021). With Vorby, we use the stories to stage a discussion and analysis of what these consequences can subsequently mean for our structures, the systems and their logics.

When we initiate a dialogue *in* the future that we dream of and strive for, backcasting to the present and discovering the alternative pathways for the future becomes achievable. Vorby is an excellent example of how to provide a shared vision of what should be in place and helps identify new stepping stones now, tomorrow and next year as paths out of the systemic deadlock towards the preferred future.

As mentioned, Vorby functions as a tangible and relatable manifestation of the new narrative, which the many actors who have contributed can take with them and invite others into so that even more people can be engaged and mobilized around the agenda of thriving youth. Vorby provides a scaffold by defining the initial contours of a future – not too detailed or thoroughly explained. The city map is not finished; it is only partially sketched. It leaves room for further development and for others to be inspired to explore new corners of the map.

Thus, the preferred future is tangible, desirable, but still incomplete: 'It's better to prefer incompleteness over completeness; capacious imagination instead of futures that are too specific or neat; and experimentation and exploration over visions and blueprints', as Mulgan underlines (2022). Building new narratives needs room for interpretation and emergent kindred stories.

To wrap up, today, Vorby is an active and relevant resource used in various initiatives by partners and other stakeholders. The entire resource of stories, films, 'choose your own adventure' and city map can be openly accessed online.

Vorby, a virtual future city, is just one way to create a shared narrative around a preferred future. And we encourage all pathfinders to find different ways of creating a new story. Importantly Vorby highlights the significance of avoiding the simplification of direction and narrative into a single catchy sentence or an unattainable utopia.

It is essential to recognize that a narrative alone does not suffice but must guide actions, experiments and learning. It is through these actions and common sensemaking that the narrative evolves over time, and we are able to fine-tune it in reciprocity. Our shared narrative is dynamic and must be renegotiated and further developed as we move forward.

Moreover, Vorby exemplifies the power of storytelling. Human beings have always told stories as part of our culture to connect us and preserve culture and traditions. Storytelling not only gives us the opportunity to connect across generations and citizen groups, it enables future generations' voices to be present. Furthermore, storytelling can also include non-human voices and influence our stories and interpretation. We will return to this perspective in the coming navigation point.

Seeing the bigger picture

Contrary to what many people believe, we do not use alternative outcomes of the future to predict the future. As we have already stated, the future is uncertain and imprecise; therefore, trying to predict it is imprecise and not very useful.

Instead, we do it to:

- Uncover our blind spots and inform the basis for decision making. To see what we are not seeing: massive and decisive threats or fantastic opportunities and new markets. Thereby, it serves as a profound basis for new policies, strategies, partnerships and business models. By testing our possible solutions in different hypothetical contexts, as the four scenarios of Boxing Future Health, we can heighten the awareness of strengths and weaknesses that we would not otherwise have detected.
- Open the conversation through a common frame of reference across multiple stakeholders and actors. By pushing some significant issues way ahead of us into the future, it becomes easier to talk about. If we are discussing matters in 2050, it is less sensitive than talking about next year or the next five.

- Create empathy for future generations. Scenarios or futures design can stretch our empathy for people living in the future. An ability that is highly needed when engaging with the long-term profound challenges we have described. When you hear a person talk about their life, it often reminds you of something in your own life – it sparks an immediate human reaction, empathy, from which you can speak and explore.
- Enable us to work long-term. Futures design empowers us to stay in the long perspectives, 10–20–30 years from now, and insist on the long-term gains that may not be measured or harvested before the next election period.
- Mobilize our imagination to discover new paths, get inspired to think radically differently, and find new ways to address the wicked problem. It helps us expand the opportunity space. When we explore multiple, diverse alternative futures, we push the boundaries of what we can imagine. This can open our eyes to entirely new possibilities and risks.
- Reframing the purpose of the systems. When we give life to alternative realities and their systems and logics, the logics of our system become more apparent. Invisible mechanisms, power relations and relationships that we never imagined could be different suddenly become visible, and we can actively challenge them and think about them differently. Without this awareness, we risk building systems that reproduce existing problems.
- Building a solid and thorough foundation with multiple perspectives, from which we can negotiate and converge, to set a clear direction towards a shared, desired future, the preferred future.

Integrating futures design and imagination in your work

We realize that an initiative such as Boxing Future Health or Vorby is unusual in its comprehensiveness. Not all organizations will have the capacity, resources and skills to venture into this kind of *worldbuilding* exercise. Our focus here is the importance of the explorative and imaginative process of engaging with futures, how it sparks your imagination and develops new ideas about possible futures that may inspire you to question, challenge, rethink and explore the present with different eyes.

By applying the methods and approaches described in the navigation point, we aim to foster a culture and practice that actively engages with futures and change. Continuously. This means being constantly aware of new opportunities and challenges and being able to act dynamically and proactively – more on this in the coming navigation point, *Navigating Balance*.

There are several great ways and open resources accessible from all over the world that you can explore if you want to engage with thought-provoking visions or literature on futures. We are inspired by the wonderful work of Tobias Revell, Stuart Candy, Anab Jain and Rob Hopkins, just to mention a few. You can also work with less high-fidelity future resources, to just get people started thinking about different futures – for example, writing simple short stories from future personas or playing imagination games such as Stuart Candy's *A Thing from the Future*.

What we have learned so far: navigating a new story

At this point, we have touched upon the importance and necessity of imagination for us to thrive as individuals and as a creative and collective force within our organizations, between organizations, and in collaboration with different stakeholders. We have learned that imagination is crucial to uncover new pathways from wicked problems.

By understanding the notion of wicked problems and systems mechanisms, we have trained our awareness of what drives systems and societal challenges today and directed our focus towards how to imagine and reframe societal structures to allow for new narratives to arise.

We have looked at ways to rehabilitate our imagination through domains such as strategic foresight, alternative futures, design and storytelling, and dived into concrete immersive experiences, showcasing how it holds immense power that can create a collective sense of purpose across diverse groups of people, organizations, positions and agendas.

Boxing Future Health showed us the massive power of 'bringing the future to life', allowing us to explore different futures first-hand, as humans and as a collective – what will a completely different future entail? Vorby underpinned the value of creating a shared common direction, the preferred future that repurposes the system around mental health. It provides a way to jointly explore and question the present and reveal new paths forward.

Creating new narratives and utilizing creative processes and methods that translate the abstract into something tangible invites and enables many more to join the conversation. It democratizes the dialogue around our future and provides many more resources for imagining and finding solutions.

The navigation point demonstrates to us as pathfinders that it is feasible to work proactively with our imagination and that there are multiple tools we can use to train, spark and mobilize it.

With well-founded reason, you might have the impression that this is a sequential process: we first identify the system's materials and the four keys, as outlined by Leadbeater and Winhall, then use future scenarios, and finally outline a preferred future to blaze new trails. However, the future is dynamic, messy and iterative, just like reality is.

Navigating balance

On a warm summer morning in 2024, I (Sara) am biking towards a conference centre outside of Copenhagen to give a presentation and conduct a workshop about the future of healthcare, imagination and how we can tackle wicked problems. I am on my way to meet a group of leaders from a large Danish hospital. On the way, my phone rings. One of the hospital section directors is calling. She wants to inform me that there was an unpleasant incident involving some of her colleagues in one of the wards the day before. A patient, in the process of detoxification, had become highly aggressive and threatened the staff with a knife. Several of the leader's staff are shaken and upset by the violent incident and are afraid to go to work.

She does not want to cancel and prefers to go ahead. She insists the organization needs to focus on the long-term perspective as well as handling the immediate, short-term issues. As she said:

> Of course, this is urgent, and we are in the middle of handling it, but there are constantly urgent severe problems we need to tackle. But if we never look up, how do we know we are heading in the right direction? Are we seeing what we are not seeing?

As the section director insists on holding this somewhat uncomfortable tension and paying attention to the long-term change, it also puts things into perspective for me. As much as I pioneer long-term thinking and the importance of focusing on the future, this severe matter affects me. I do not want to belittle their experiences. I do not want to come across as ignorant, unaware of the importance of the present.

This story and reflection materialize from a particular situation that one of us, Sara, experienced back in 2024. The case underlines exactly the necessity and importance of acknowledging the different balances leaders and pathfinders find themselves having to navigate in.

The fact is that the urgency of immediate, present problems pushes long-term issues and crises further into the horizon and to the backs of our minds. And if that continues, we never manage to change the dominant structures and logics, we never transform the systems and solve the problems. That is why we must be able to maintain the tension between the present and the future. We must have the ability to navigate these balances.

While the navigation point *Navigating a New Story* directs us towards alternative futures and encourages pathfinders to ignite their imagination in creating strategic directionality for our work, this navigation point, *Navigating Balance*, places us with an outset in the present. Here, we are faced with the tricky dilemmas of striving towards a preferred future while working in the midst of the challenges, structures and logics of the present.

4

Holding the tension between opposing attitudes

In *Navigating Balance*, we uncover the many dilemmas that lie inherent in navigating societal change: Heading towards the future, while interfering with the present. Seeing changes evolve slowly over time but working quickly to create progress. Grasping large complex and abstract problems, while breaking them down into smaller, concrete actions. Impatiently stimulating change yet patiently waiting to understand the bigger picture. Being speculative of what the future might bring, but rational about the challenges we face.

These are examples of the different ways of working – we call them attitudes – that one, as a pathfinder, must be able to embrace and even switch between when working with societal change processes. Navigating in societal transition means placing oneself in the middle of multiple tensions: holding incoherent and sometimes unaligned attitudes that pull us in different and often seemingly opposite directions.

In Figure 4.1 you can see a visual overview of these opposing attitudes, following our elaboration on their inherent dilemmas.

The point here is that neither of these attitudes and ways of working are worse or better than the other. With the navigation point *Navigating Balance*, we argue that all pathfinders must accept the noisy path of balancing different and opposing attitudes in their work and mindset and it is an absolute prerequisite for progress that we can juggle between them.

Figure 4.1: Opposing attitudes

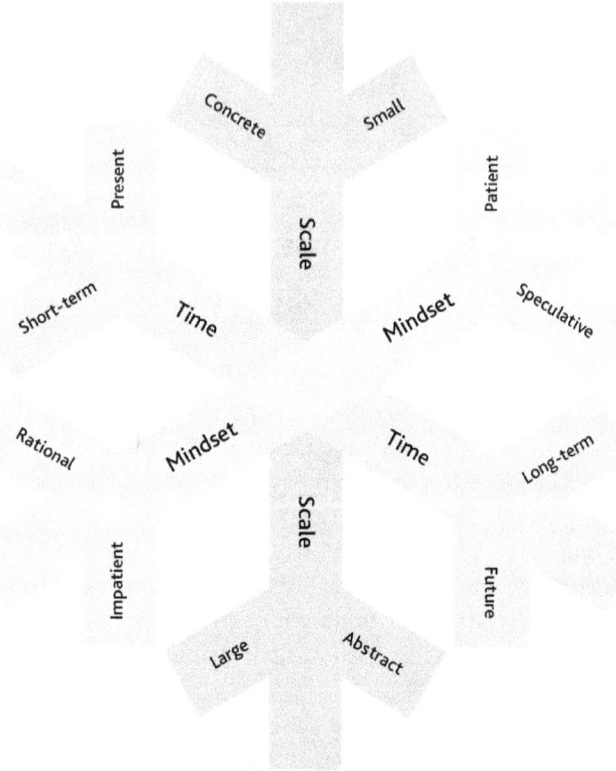

Note: The image of opposing attitudes draws inspiration from the creation of a snowflake. We argue that pathfinders should embrace the opposing attitudes simultaneously, just as the different branches of a snowflake grow synchronously and symmetrically.

Tension in time

We experience a constant, inherent tension in time that we must be able to navigate when working with societal change. The tension in time is a natural consequence of how societal change slowly unfolds over several decades. We might not harvest the fruits of the change and impact we want to create before decades have passed. We, as pathfinders, might not even live it to see it through. At the same time, societal change demands rapid action. This is the case with climate change that demands accelerated action today if we are to keep the temperature from rising above 1.5°C in 2050 as agreed in the Paris Agreement. It calls for the ability to work towards long-term change by constantly delivering on short-term actions targeting that change.

Our awareness of the long-term perspective in time is not only a one-directional orientation towards the future, but also a view of the past. What inventions, achievements and developments, such as women's right to vote, women entering the labour market and the development of the iPhone, have influenced, for example, the welfare society, with schools, kindergartens, nursing homes and digital social services as we know it today? How might we learn from the past as we build our future?

Tension in scale

We experience a tension in scale and levels of abstraction. Our grand systemic challenges, such as global warming, loss of biodiversity, plastic in the ocean, a growing ageing population, the declining birth rate in significant parts of the world, or the growing number of young people not thriving, are problems that all seem to be coming at us with the force of a tsunami.

Systemic problems like these are so large, wild and unruly that they are impossible to control and work with. They must be broken down into smaller problems, fenced in and tamed so that we can interact with them. Yet, as we zoom in on a problem and its solution, we reduce the complexity. We become prone to miss some of the critical dimensions of a problem and how these dimensions interact with each other and the larger system as a whole. We might even reproduce some of the problems that we initially set out to solve!

These unwanted results are referred to as 'rebound effects': intentionally good-hearted actions with a backward effect. A good example of this can be found in McKinsey's *The State of Fashion 2022* report (McKinsey & Company, 2022), which reveals a disturbing trend in fashion. It shows that despite the growth of the second-hand market, the demand for new clothing continues to rise. The numbers imply a potential risk that the success of second-hand platforms enables consumers to quickly sell off new clothes they have barely worn to pay for new styles. Hence, resell platforms intentionally initiated to slow down the rapid production of new fashion items could potentially enable the exact opposite – an increase in consumption. Rebound effects are, therefore, a constant reminder to constantly zoom in and out – to look at how the result of one intervention affects the broader system – and vice versa.

Tension in mindset

Working with different approaches to time, scale and levels of abstraction inevitably also means working with different mindsets. The long-term systemic work of understanding the societal drivers and slowly but surely mobilizing these in the preferred direction demands that we remain patient, calm and curious. We also need to acknowledge that the effects of our actions happen slowly over time and are affected by a mix of events outside of our control. At times, when we feel a pressing need to act fast, we must do the opposite: take a step back to think, explore and challenge our assumptions about the problem. Patience should not be mistaken for apathy – being patient does not equal doing nothing.

Yet, there still is a need for impatience when working to change the course of these untamed societal challenges. However, we need to be mindful that there are nuances to that impatience. The impatience for results in the here and now must go hand-in-hand with a persistent impatience that pushes us to test our assumptions through actions, drive people forward quickly, build momentum and insist on urgency.

Another mindset tension we personally try to balance throughout this book is the tension between a speculative and a rational mindset. As we have covered, we stress the need to ignite our imagination and creativity to envision and speculate about a better future, to create a new and compelling narrative about this future so we have something to strive for. But if we fail to turn the speculations of the future into actions of today, we ignore the context we navigate in. And then we cannot get a proper grip on what drives change forward.

We envision these competing mindsets as an inner battle that we as pathfinders have to hold, maintaining an acceptance of the potentially rivalling states within our inner self.

Embracing the tension

We observe how different people or different types of organizations feel more comfortable in either one of the two mindset extremes. In our experience, a majority of institutions and companies today lean towards the short-term, rational and concrete. At the same time, some actors, such as innovators, researchers and futurists, thrive on the opposite end of the spectrum. They are driven by long-term, abstract and speculative transformation. We find that our inability to drive societal change relates to this separation of these two different attitudes by different societal actors and roles. The lack of connection between the two groups and their respective mindsets renders changes difficult because the two factions tend to focus their energy on advocating for one mindset in opposition to the other when we really should be working together to embrace both.

All the different attitudes are vital in societal transformation. Therefore, the unique task for the pathfinder is to create and maintain a space where this tension of opposing attitudes and the orchestration of the continuous zooming in and out of time, space and mindset can be utilized to push development forward.

It is, therefore, paramount for us as pathfinders to build up the necessary dynamic capabilities to balance this tension, so that the abstract informs the concrete, the long-term informs the short-term, and vice versa. While some people may be better at one mindset than the other, we insist that the interplay and interaction between opposing mindsets must be continuously orchestrated.

In her excellent book on planetary design, Engholm argues for *high amplitude thinking* (Engholm, 2023), meaning that the bigger the amplitude, that is, the distance between the micro and the macro perspective, the more we can take radical decisions that can potentially gain more impact. Engholm encourages us to think big and reflect on the grand implication of our actions while we hyper-focus on specific, concrete interventions. Thus, zooming in on the concrete and tangible actions all the way out to the larger and systemic effects and societal consequences and vice versa.

In our conversation with strategic designer Brian Frandsen, he challenged the dominant perception that these different attitudes conflict. He suggests that this idea of opposites is grounded in the dominating culture and institutional practice today that puts value on implementation and fast-paced decisions. Furthermore, he points to the fact that the discrepancy between opposing extremes is not necessarily a given. Paradoxes or contradictions are well known in the designer's field of work: creating both function *and* aesthetics, achieving simplicity and user-friendliness *and* handling high complexity in a product or service, or catering to individual needs *and* addressing the demands of the community. As Frandsen puts it: 'Some people thrive in this tension, especially designers, and more people can learn to embrace this tension' (Frandsen, 2024).

Creativity thrives on contradictions; therefore, these opposing attitudes must be welcomed as a 'both-and' mindset, enabling innovation and radical ideas to sprout. It is not a choice you have to make, but a blessing in disguise. The tension drives us as pathfinders to create, explore and remain flexible in our search for new answers.

One might gain inspiration from biological cycles, observing how they operate naturally in the interplay between different attitudes – from slow and patient growth over the course of many years with the composting of trees and the development of large landscapes to the quick and transient life cycles of insects and flowers.

Throughout this navigation point on balances, we look for ways to navigate in and embrace this tension of attitudes. We will explore:

- How the design mindset can help us navigate in the *in-between* and the *both-and*.
- How we might work for long-term change in a short-term world.
- How mission-oriented innovation provides a framework for orchestrating this balancing between scales.

- How portfolios let us acknowledge the complexity and break it down into smaller bits so we can practically manage this tension.

Navigating the in-between and the both-and

> It is the particular, productive interaction between thinking and doing that is the hallmark of a design approach. (Engholm, 2023)

As design practitioners, we have experienced first-hand how design as a way of working and organizing processes can be a helpful partner in navigating this somewhat schizophrenic dance between attitudes.

At its core, design thinking organizes iterative processes of shifts in attitude between a convergent and a divergent mindset. Thus, design provides us with processes we can implement to move swiftly between different attitudes. This process is best put into form in the acknowledged *double diamond model* (see Figure 4.2) initially developed by the British Design Council in 2004. It is a simple visual representation of an innovation process that moves between divergent and convergent ways of working. *Divergent* thinking is a creative, free-flowing and open mode of exploring many possible solutions, *convergent* thinking focuses on organizing and structuring ideas using logic to analyse and prioritize the best solutions.

Industrial design thinking was successfully applied to facilitate innovation processes that advanced the development of innovative solutions in business and the public sector, spearheaded by the American design agency IDEO in the late 1990s. Over the last decade, design thinking has been criticized for its too narrow and sometimes shallow focus on solution design: creating products and services that might address a user need, but fail to understand the system and societal challenges around these needs (Iskander, 2018). Yet, several thinkers, such as design practitioner and researcher Christian Bason, expand the concept of and the application of design, stressing how it can play an essential and more holistic role for systems change (Bason and Skibsted, 2022).

Figure 4.2: Double diamond

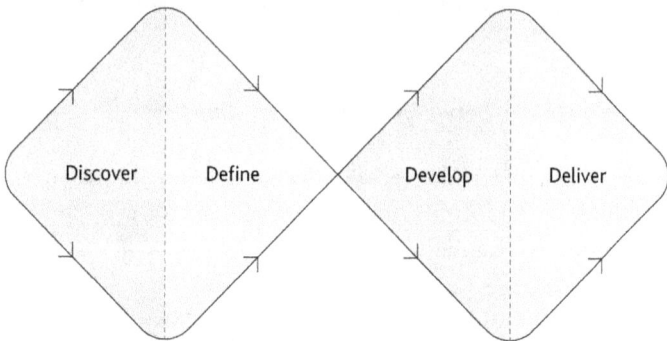

Note: In the double diamond the 'discover' and 'develop' phase are *divergent* phases indicated by the arrows opening. And the 'define' and 'develop' phases are *convergent* phases where the arrows narrow in.

Source: Design Council (2004)

Perhaps due to this criticism, the British Design Council revisited and adapted their famous double diamond in 2021 to introduce *The Systemic Design Framework* that takes the climate crisis as a point of departure and accentuates how design has the capability to address and solve systemic sustainability challenges. Through several interviews they explored the characteristics of sustainable change makers and described four new spheres for system-led design that widen the traditional double diamond.

The four spheres are: (1) orientation and vision setting; (2) connections and relationships; (3) leadership and storytelling; (4) continuing the journey (see Figure 4.3).

Additionally, they described four critical roles for designers who operate in these spheres and who lead the way in systems change. Notably, these four roles align well with the four navigation points that guide this book. Our perspective is that the pathfinders take on these four roles when addressing societal challenges. Sometimes simultaneously, sometimes overlapping, other times sequentially.

The four roles are:

- *System thinker*: someone who has the ability to see how everything is interconnected in a bigger picture and zoom

between the micro and the macro and across silos (what we explore in *Navigating Balance*).
- *Leader and storyteller*: someone who can tell a great story about what might be possible and why this is important, get buy-in from all levels and have the tenacity to see the work through (these are points we made in *Navigating a New Story*).
- *Designer and maker*: someone who understands the power of design and innovation tools, has the technical and creative skills to make things happen, and makes sure they are used early in the work (we'll see this role unfold in *Navigating Experiments*).
- *Connector and convener*: someone with good relationships who can create spaces where people from different backgrounds come together and join the dots to create a bigger movement (as explored in *Navigating Interdependence*).

Figure 4.3: The Systemic Design Framework

Source: Design Council (2021)

We appreciate how this revised model widens the original scope of the double diamond and illustrates the different dimensions that must be added to a traditional innovation process to accommodate for navigating societal change.

The essential point is that the designerly way of working and thinking cultivates a way to continuously shift between attitudes, to zoom in and out of time, space and scale while never leaving any of the attitudes behind. In this way, some attitudes will be more prominent and saturated at certain times, while others fade into the background.

A planetary perspective

Engholm has extended the design thinking model even further. In her book *Design for a New World* she adds an extra layer – a *planetary perspective* – to all design decisions so that we do not only reflect on the inherent systemic opportunities and consequences of our actions but also on the effects our decisions may have on 'the oceans, the fauna, the flora and the human race' (Engholm, 2023).

Engholm's insistence on humanity's responsibility towards the planet is not isolated. We experience a growing movement within design, environmental and systems thinking, for us as humans to acknowledge our interdependence of nature. In some cases, humans are even perceived as nature's humble servant instead of its master.

Planetary design challenges the traditional human-centred approach in design and recognizes the agency of non-human entities like animals, plants and ecosystems. Thus, forcing us to broaden our attention span beyond just humans and human-made systems and design with multiple species' needs and perspectives in mind.

There are various emerging theories and frameworks, such as interspecies design, multispecies design, planet-centred design or eco-centric design, with the overarching idea of incorporating the needs of animals and plants into the design process. Here, there are several examples of designers who address the well-being of other species.

The design studio Superflux has developed a speculative multispecies banquet where humans, animals, plants and fungi have an equal seat at the table. Their job is to carve out a new world from the smouldering remains of the old. After surviving Earth's abrupt shift to an era of precarious climate, this multispecies community gathers in the ruins of modernity to find new ways of living together and revive the land (Superflux, 2021). Another example is the agency WeDoDemocracy, who carry out democratic innovation and deliberation processes by considering future generations and justifying their voice, by always leaving a chair free for those who, with good reason, cannot represent their perspective in person. We follow this paradigm shift with great curiosity and eagerness as it allows us to fundamentally rethink our role and responsibility as pathfinders.

Working for long-term change in a short-term world

> Taking the long view is about collapsing the distance between now and then, today and tomorrow, this century and the next. (Bason and Skibsted, 2022)

Let us return to the initial dilemma of opposing attitudes and take a deep dive into the notion of *time*. We acknowledge that the challenges, such as transitioning to a circular economy or fighting plastics in the ocean, take time. Systems, incentives, nature's processes, technological development and human behaviour must evolve for the transition to be accomplished.

We build on Engholm's take on systems, as she states, the system mindset

> is based on a notion of the interconnectedness of all things, and thus also on a cyclical notion of time in which every action has consequences: what we send out into the world is what we get back; what we do now will cause ripple effects in both the short- and the long-term future. (Engholm, 2023: 226)

Hence, maintaining a constant gaze far into the horizon is a prerequisite when working with societal transition.

It is a well-known fact of the climate crisis that our failure to act now will affect generations in the future. Just skim through one of the many reports from the Intergovernmental Panel on Climate Change that publish knowledge on climate change, its causes, potential impacts and response options. However, we still struggle to integrate the needs of future generations in our planning today. Some may argue that our failure to act and respond to future crises, such as the climate crisis, is due to its abstract and distant nature. It is hard for us to grasp and relate to problems that seem so far away from many of us in space and time.

On top of this, many of the structures in society are simply not geared towards the long-term view. You might argue that we are stuck in a short-term world where organizations have built incentives for us to deliver short-term results.

'Short-sighted thinking has become an existential threat to humanity, particularly in politics, business, and society, where the demand is for quick results to either win re-election or meet quarterly financial targets', say Striegler and Buhelt (2023). Yet, they also point out that thinking in a longer time span, even across several generations, is not a novel idea.

Indigenous cultures such as the Haudenosaunee Confederacy in northeastern America have been known to apply a 'seven generation principle' for centuries, considering how their decisions will affect the following seven generations. It is put beautifully in Law 28 of the Constitution of the Iroquois Nation: 'Look and listen for the welfare of the whole people and have always in view not only the present but also the coming generations, even those whose faces are yet beneath the surface of the ground' (Indigenous People, 2016). The rituals and values of Indigenous culture challenge the often winning argument in Western society that issues too far out of our human proximity or time span are too abstract and distant for us to deal with. A consciousness about history and other cultures' thinking ensures that long-term thinking and planning principles can be learned.

We see several sparkles of counter-reactions to our society's short attention span. In the business sector, Paul Polman, former CEO of Unilever, created quite a stir, when he, on his first day as CEO at Unilever, announced he would abolish earnings guidance and quarterly reporting in the company. He reflected that: 'People often behave short-term because of the boundaries that are put around them. ... It's clear that the issues like climate change or inequality or food securities or these enormous opportunities out there can really not be solved in the rat race of short-term reporting' says Polman in his 2021 book *Net Positive – How courageous companies thrive by giving more than they take*.

Polman launched the ten-year Unilever Sustainable Living Plan, which sought to decouple the company's growth from its environmental footprint. Moving away from quarterly reporting allowed the company to make long-term investments that span longer periods. And it served to support a cultural shift as well as a shift in mindset where focus moved from the race for quick wins to an impact-driven culture. As a side note, some studies show that companies perform better financially when they report annually instead of quarterly to their shareholders (American Accounting Association, 2018). Thus, the insistence on the long term can also be an economically sound decision.

In the political sphere, we have seen the rise of Future Committees in Finland, Iceland, Paraguay, Uruguay, Chile, the Philippines and Lithuania in an attempt to heighten the political focus on issues and challenges that are placed far out in the horizon, but that will affect the well-being of the nation and the citizens in the future. These committees' job has been to produce reports and policy recommendations that contain long-term perspectives, goals and proposals for future development (Striegler and Buhelt, 2023).

Wales stands out as a particularly progressive country in this matter. In 2015, Wales introduced the *Well-being of Future Generations Act*. Part of the act was to appoint a Future Generation Commissioner in 2016, a position Derek Walker holds as we write this. The law legally obliges public bodies to do five things:

1. take account of the long term;
2. prevent problems from occurring or getting worse;
3. take an integrated approach;
4. take a collaborative approach; and
5. consider and involve people of all ages and diversity.
   (Future Generations Commissioner of Wales, 2015)

This intergenerational approach in policy is an appealing counterpoint to the political pressure we have grown accustomed to in many cases. We have all experienced situations where political decisions have been adjusted to fit within the borders of an electoral cycle or where stand-alone issues or popularity contests distract our focus from addressing the root of our societal challenges.

Nuancing time: The Three Horizons

A way to further nuance the notion of time is the Three Horizons Framework inspired by Bill Sharpe's (2020) work (see Figure 4.4), which is an excellent way to expand our thinking about time and action (Striegler and Erlendsson, 2023). It helps us increase our awareness of different frames and phases of time as well as our expectations for and planning towards the future. With this framework, we operate with three different time frames:

1. Horizon One helps us dismantle the *existing structures today* that work against the emergence of new or complementary systems.
2. Horizon Two helps us create the conditions and infrastructure necessary to facilitate and nurture the *turbulent transition* from the current system to a better one.
3. Horizon Three supports us to challenge assumptions and logics and helps us define and maintain a shared focus on what a sustainable and *preferred future* might look like.

We have covered Horizon Three, the preferred future, in the previous navigation point. It is now instructive to understand how Horizon Two helps us deal with the hard part of transitioning out of the system in crisis to the preferred future. It reveals that we cannot just jump out of one flawed system into a new and better one. To move ourselves out of the system, it is often necessary to establish temporary structures, incentives, interventions or technologies that enable society to act differently through new logics and acceptances.

Here is an example: In our efforts to achieve gender equality, we strive for a preferred future where all men and women fundamentally have the same rights and opportunities in society and are treated equally. Yet, in our efforts to get there and advance the change today, we have seen, for example, the rise of quotas

Figure 4.4: The Three Horizons Framework

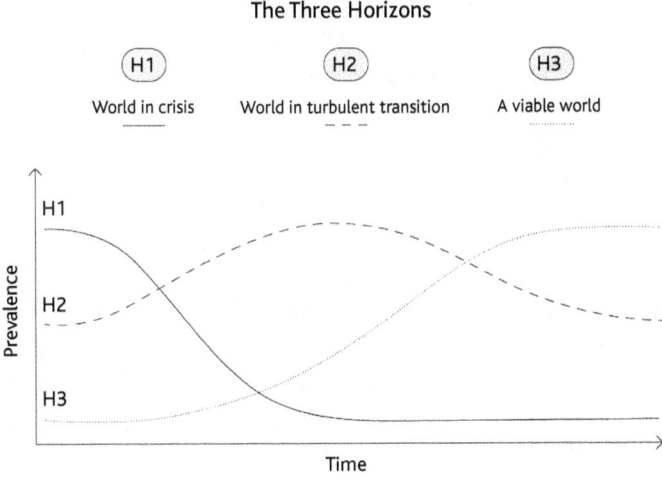

Source: Adapted from Sharpe (2020)

for women to hold board positions or earmarked parental leave for fathers. In some ways, these structural incentives defer their overall goal – our preferred future. By establishing differential treatment for women on boards or men on leave, we emphasize the difference between the genders, fundamentally challenging the initial idea of gender equality (our preferred future). Considering Horizon Two these structural changes are temporarily necessary incentives that are put in place to prompt men and women to act differently, because society has failed at other attempts to stimulate this change. This is probably because our behaviour around mothers' and fathers' roles is deeply rooted in our current understanding, structures and values. In that way, quotas and earmarked parental leave serve as enablers and, by no means, end goals. If they are successful, they can eventually be dismantled as they become obsolete. Which, eventually, will pave the way for true gender equality.

As Horizon Three gives us a clear direction of the preferred future, and Horizon Two lets new temporal initiatives and interventions grow, Horizon One reminds us to think about things we need to stop doing.

Often, when working to improve and transform a system, we are so focused on development that we overlook the need to phase out certain elements entirely. It does not make sense to keep adding layers upon layers, partly because we need to remember that something may no longer provide value, and partly because sometimes we need to remove something for other things to grow.

A compelling example comes from the Danish healthcare sector. At Lillebælt Hospital, through the *Choose Wisely* project, efforts have been made to reduce over-treatment in the healthcare system. Unnecessary scans, blood tests and check-ups, which often do not benefit the patient, are being eliminated to avoid false reassurance and unnecessary anxiety. The project focuses on providing treatments that genuinely make a difference for patients. In this process, the hospital discovered that a simple test, the urine dipstick, was routinely used to examine a urine sample for various chemical substances without this data being requested or utilized in follow-up care. The urine dipstick cannot reliably indicate whether a patient has, for example, a urinary tract infection, and this example highlights how such tests may not lead to more accurate diagnoses. Yet the urine dipstick was still frequently used (Dengsøe, 2024).

This is a good example of over-treatment, where, with the best of intentions, healthcare professionals want to help patients and might even be afraid of under-treating or making mistakes. It reveals a mindset where the belief is that the more we do, the better. According to the project, patients have developed an expectation that the more treatment and medical examinations they undergo, the more beneficial it is for them.

In this case, it seems we are culturally wired to believe that more is better – and as long as we keep adding, we do not disrupt the status quo. Thus, we fail to assess whether we are creating genuine value. Across many areas of society, not just in healthcare, we need to fundamentally rethink the notion that more is always better.

As the doctor Jakob Blaabjerg Espesen beautifully puts it, 'Sometimes, the best thing we can do for the patients is actually nothing at all' (Dengsøe, 2024).

The project has implemented this phase-out, and as a result, the use of urine dipsticks has been discontinued for many patient groups, reducing the use by 17 per cent.

The Horizon Framework's layered idea of time and transition adds nuance to our discussions about the future, forcing us not to look naively towards the preferred future, but to deal with the reality of our existing structures and to design ways to move out of them.

To conclude the issue of time, we want to encourage pathfinders to rigorously insist on the long-term perspective. To do so, we suggest scrutinizing our existing structures or systems, be it our budgeting or planning cycles, to understand how these might hinder our ability to consider the long-term. The patient view into the far future that spans across generations is a prerequisite for systems change. It is, however, not an excuse for stagnation or idleness. A long-term focus must be matched with rapid action and fast-paced results. We will dive into this as we explore the portfolio approach. But to prepare for this, we introduce the concept of mission-oriented innovation.

5

Missions: balancing top-down and bottom-up

As we work towards societal transition, we expect our readers to be painfully aware that the problems and challenges we address are always larger than us, unsolvable by one person or one organization. The wicked and systemic problems call for not one, but many solutions. And no singular organizational entity can overcome, for example, global warming or inequality alone. However, with the emergence of mission-oriented innovation, a theoretical, economic and political approach for solving large societal problems, we are presented with a framework that steers policy makers, researchers, economists, innovators and citizens together to solve our pressing crises, acknowledging their scale, their vastness and their complexity.

Here, we want to highlight some aspects of why mission-oriented innovation, to us, is a promising framework to adopt as pathfinders.

Missions create directionality

The moonshot terminology in missions, inspired by the American moon landing in 1969, encourages missions to set an ambitious direction that sometimes seem almost unattainable, and is highly relevant to society. Missions set ambitious targets to solve complex challenges, where, in many cases, we do not have complete knowledge about how to get there. Missions do not accept the many barriers or obstacles that are inherent in current dysfunctional systems. By setting the ambition, formulating the desirable North Star, they help us set the necessary direction that will mobilize us towards the preferred future.

Targeted missions drive commitment to change

Missions do not address vague and imprecise challenges or ideas, such as *sustainability* or *inequality*, but rather target their focus towards an impact we wish to achieve: for example, the Australian Drought Resilience mission that aims to build rural resilience and reduce drought impacts by 30 per cent by 2030; the Swedish government-backed Innovation Fund Vinnova's mission that all streets in Sweden will be sustainable, healthy and full of life in 2030 (Vinnova, 2021); or the European Union's cancer mission that aims to improve the lives of more than three million people by 2030 through prevention, cure and, for those affected by cancer including their families, to live longer and better lives.

These binding mission targets can drive actors across society to stay with and focus on a given impact or result. Their bold objectives push us not to stray from the path of reaching the mission, getting caught up in the complex and abstract challenges of the system today. As Piret Tõnurist from the Organisation for Economic Co-operation and Development (OECD)'s Observatory for Public Sector Innovation stresses, the mission goal trumps everything else – it creates direction, and it drives commitment: 'The goal itself is paramount. You start with it; you end with it. Whatever it takes' (Tõnurist, 2024).

Missions insist on the long term

Because of the scale and amplitude of missions, the targets we set for them are long-term and often placed far out into the future. This forces us to plan, organize and accumulate funding and resources for initiatives that span across often up to ten years or more. Thus, long-term missions provide a new political and economic framework that allows us to maintain the long-term perspective in a short-term world.

Missions include top-down and bottom-up experimentation

While mission statements are formulated as top-down goals often produced by politicians, philanthropies or other people in power, missions are designed to be developed and implemented through the interaction between bottom-up and top-down stakeholders across industry, research, government and civil society to develop shared solutions (Mazzucato, 2018a). The framework behind mission-oriented innovation is designed to leverage innovation and resources across society around the joint mission. Therefore, missions reveal a more holistic and cross-sectoral approach to transformation that recognizes the power of bottom-up experimentation among multiple societal actors.

While the moon landing is often brought forward as an example of a mission, several people, Mazzucato and us included, argue that the challenges we target our missions towards today, such as the European Commission's mission to cure cancer or our efforts to achieve a carbon neutral society, are more wicked and complex than bringing humans to the moon. The moon landing was complicated but not wicked.

This sentiment is not new. In 1977, Richard Nelson opened his book *The Moon and the Ghetto* with the provocative question, 'If we can land a man on the moon, why can't we solve the problems of the ghetto?' (Nelson, 1977).

A critical view on missions

We recognize that, in many cases, the promise of mission-oriented innovation is bigger than its implementation in practice. The development of the framework has been characterized by quite the hype in political circles. It is an emerging theory and field with lacking methodology and practice. Due to the inherent long-term perspective, we are still waiting to fully harvest the output and the impact of this new approach.

The OECD Observatory for Public Sector Innovation has published the report *13 Reasons Why Missions Fail* that sheds light on the many causes for unsuccessful missions (Tõnurist, 2023). Among them is *mission washing* – the political hype for mission-oriented innovation has led several organizations to adopt the terminology without adopting its practice, or *orphan missions*, examples of cross-governmental missions, where the ownership behind the mission is lacking.

Moreover, we have encountered several critical voices of Mariana Mazzucato's take on missions that bring important nuances to the debate. For instance, questioning the state's ability to drive change widely across society. In our conversation with writer and systems thinker Jon Alexander, Co-founder of the New Citizen Project, he expressed his scepticism on how state-driven missions direct their focus primarily on mobilizing institutions and private sector resources and fail in driving citizen participation and engagement around missions:

> What about all the people? We need everyone. What if you opened missions to the ideas, energy and resources of all of the public, starting with what people in communities are already doing? Think community energy, community food, solidarity-based healthcare systems, and more. … And then governance too: what if you had citizen assemblies be part of the governance of missions? Then you'd really be doing missions with people, not for them or to them. (Alexander, 2024)

Exactly which label we put on our work with societal change is not that important. We are more concerned with how we work with it than what we call it. However, despite the inherent challenges of missions, we have, practically, experienced that the framework and methodology behind missions can be powerful as means to enhance the focus on a more impact-driven and system-critical approach to implementing change. Importantly, we find that a mission-oriented approach provides us with tools and ways to master the tension between attitudes. Let us explore how.

Innovation turned upside down

In many ways, missions imply an upside-down approach to innovation compared to what we have grown accustomed to in 'traditional' innovation practice. Figure 5.1 illustrates traditional

Figure 5.1: The Megaphone Model

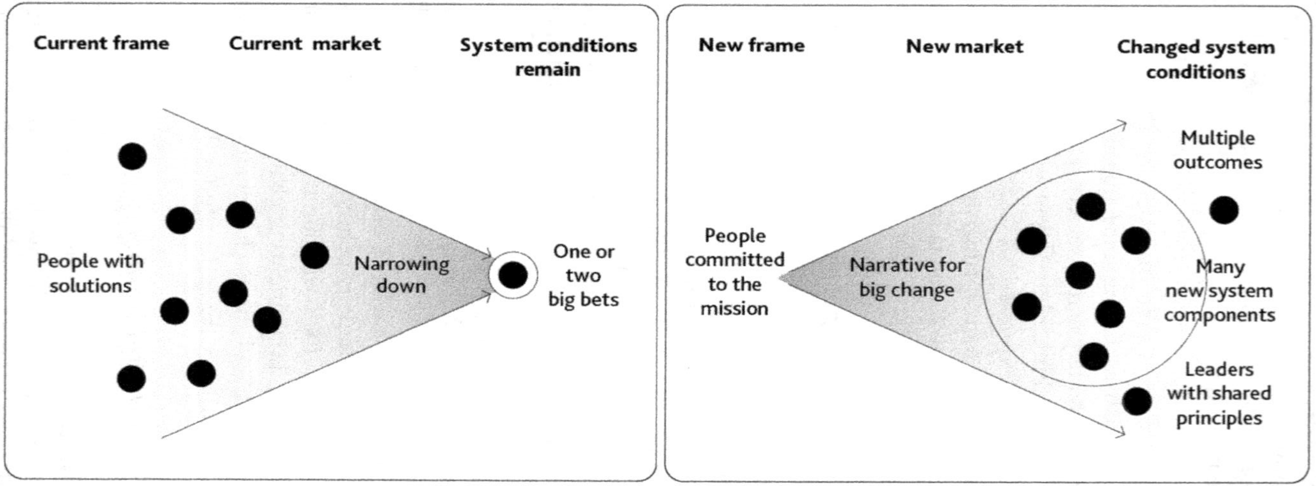

Source: Adapted from ALT/NOW (2018); published by Conway et al (2019)

innovation – here visualized as a funnel, and the mission approach – a megaphone.

The model illustrates the difference between traditional innovation processes that focus on developing solutions within the existing system (funnel) and processes that aim to change the system (megaphone). Within mission-oriented innovation, the focus is on setting a shared, ambitious direction for multiple solutions that will bring us multiple outcomes on our path towards the preferred future. As illustrated, the narrative for change guides the initiatives, interventions and experiments in the mission. The right side of Figure 5.1 also illustrates that the governance task of missions is to steer a portfolio of projects and interventions over a longer time span to radically improve value creation (Bason and Striegler, 2023).

This 'upside-down' approach of missions calls for a new innovative practice that demands us to develop new skills in public and private organizations. This shift in practice is illustrated in Table 5.1.

Since missions have spun out as a new political and economic practice, often instigated by big political institutions such as the European Commission, nation-states or city administrations, it can seem overwhelming as an individual pathfinder in an organization or business with a smaller political and economic mandate, how to latch on to this movement.

This has also been our experience with our work in a small organization such as the Danish Design Center (DDC) – an organization consisting of approximately 40 people with limited power over some of the major agendas it contributes to (such as the circular transition or the mental health and well-being of young people). It is an essential point with missions that they are collaborative and bottom-up initiatives – some nation-wide, some confined to the borders of a city or region. We do not necessarily wish to encourage businesses and organizations worldwide to start launching several *new* missions, but rather to understand how one can contribute to or enrich existing missions through partnerships and alliances. This is something we will uncover in the final navigation point, *Navigating Interdependence*.

All kinds of organizations can be mission-oriented. We see universities, corporations, companies, philanthropic institutions

Table 5.1: Traditional innovation versus mission-oriented innovation

Traditional innovation	Mission-oriented innovation
Problem and solution focus *We work with one problem with the aim to develop one solution*	Opportunity focus *We create an opportunity space with several components and multiple solutions*
We work in the present towards the future *Solutions are developing within the boundaries of the existing system*	We place ourselves in the future *Solutions are developed to create new and better future systems*
Project focus *Focus is on the performance and result of a project*	Portfolio focus *Focus is on the interplay between projects and how they inform the overall mission*
Competition *The aim is to beat competitors in the market*	Collaboration *We are dependent on and seek alliances with partners across the ecosystem*
Governance is an expense *Expenses for governance in project are kept at a minimum*	Governance is an investment *We invest time and resources for partners and stakeholders to collaborate and transfer knowledge*
Limited evaluation reports *Projects are evaluated through midterm and final evaluation reports*	Learning and monitoring is an everyday practice *Continuous learning loops and knowledge sharing are integrated in and across the projects*
Closed innovation teams *Innovation teams operate internally within the organization*	Open 'third places' *Innovation and knowledge transfer happen through open and interdisciplinary 'third places'*

and innovation institutes that either define themselves as mission-driven, develop missions or contribute to existing societal missions. Collaboration around missions creates the opportunity for smaller organizations to access resources, knowledge and skills in driving larger societal transformation. Therefore, the mission-oriented approach should hold significant opportunities for both small and large organizations from both public and private sectors.

A portfolio approach

As mentioned, mission-oriented innovation finally lets us work long-term. And a mission portfolio provides a structure for organizing this work, operating across different scales of small and big, abstract and concrete.

Portfolio management is the dynamic process of managing multiple activities in a combined framework. Think of it as a dashboard of the mission's many ongoing activities that allow the pathfinder to plan, observe and monitor the individual activities and their interaction.

The activities in a mission portfolio unfold in the dynamic interplay between top-down goals, policies, and frameworks and bottom-up initiatives and experimentation from businesses, civil society and public organizations. As illustrated in the *megaphone model*, mission entails a myriad of smaller solutions – components – that move the system forward through their interplay.

Let us provide a simple example: if a mission sets out to take a human being to the moon and return them safely to earth, the success of the mission depends on the interaction between many different solutions and the innovation across several sectors: The building of a rocket, the training of astronauts, the planning of the route, the invention of new materials, the design of space suits, the preparation of long-lasting, nutritious food for space, and the development of communication technology, and so on. Several tests and trials have been discarded to reach this goal.

In July 1969 the Americans succeeded and the mission was accomplished. It was achieved due to the successful combination of the many different components. Each of them is separately designed and developed towards that common goal. It acquired seven years of enormous investment, risk-taking, new technologies, interventions, collaborations and partnerships. It was bold, ambitious and dangerous.

Structuring the portfolio

There is no one way of designing portfolios – they should relate to the specific challenge and context you operate in. As Piret Tõnurist put it in our conversation with her: 'The goal of the mission is so ambitious and impactful that it allows you the luxury of designing a bespoke structure for that mission' (Tõnurist, 2024).

The OECD's Observatory of Public Sector Innovation has worked extensively with portfolios. As they uncover in their

2022 report on *Innovation Portfolios*, the portfolio approach can be helpful for several purposes (OECD, 2022):

- Avoid objectification helping us reveal the collective impact of the different projects.
- Tackle risk aversion, allowing us to assess the bigger picture of a wide range of projects and to distribute resources and risk in multiple directions.
- Identify synergies between activities, exploring how activities could be linked or form the basis of collaborative relationships.
- Build value chains and support scaling by considering the entire innovation value chain.
- Monitor activities in many layers connected to big reforms: portfolios can be analysed at the team unit, an organizational and a broader ecosystem level to assess the desired strategic impacts.
- Plan across ecosystems spanning several sectors and necessitate the alignment of innovation activities across ecosystems.
- Avoid lock-in and capture by innovation fads, maintaining an open-ended and interconnected approach to innovation, by-passing pre-determined rigid, linear and logic models and pathways to solutions.

Overseeing a mission portfolio makes substantial demands on how portfolios are managed and governed. Here, the person or people in charge of the missions, the pathfinders, must *assure directionality*, keeping a constant focus on the mission target, *maintain a systemic approach* by integrating projects and stakeholders across value chains, sectors and knowledge domains to leverage innovation and cross-pollination. And finally, to *ensure continuous learning and adaptation* so that learning, data and insights from across the portfolio inform new initiatives, new partnership and alterations of existing projects (Bason and Striegler, 2023).

An adaptive portfolio: Decoupling 2030

From our experience we have learned how mission-oriented portfolios challenge many traditional governance models and project structures. Therefore, we have been keen to experiment with how to build governance models around missions that both incentivize long-term initiatives as well as make room for rapid experimentation. Thus, a governance that embraces multiple attitudes.

In a close collaboration between the DDC, the Danish philanthropy: The Danish Industry Foundation and five other organizations, a unique opportunity to explore precisely this blossomed: A partnership that led to the launch of the eight-year mission-oriented programme Decoupling 2030.

In short, Decoupling 2030 sets out to radically accelerate the sustainable transition of the manufacturing industry in Denmark, setting a mission goal to, over the course of eight years, move 650 Danish manufacturing companies up a maturity-ladder within sustainability, ensuring a significant reduction of their environmental footprint through reduction of CO_2, water use, resources, energy and waste.

While the ambition for the mission was clear, the process for how to get there was more open-ended and exploratory. The partnership behind the mission, consisting of six organizations, DDC included, were uncertain of what interventions, tools, mechanism and steps to set in motion to get there. Having worked extensively with sustainability, the partner group had strong ideas about where to start and how to prioritize – but they also acknowledged that the field of sustainable transition is in constant development. There are barriers we have yet to understand. Technological and societal developments around us affect the change in ways we cannot predict eight years down the line. Therefore, creating a mission that left room and space to constantly learn and adapt to insights was essential. It had to be easy to make changes in activities and focus areas, but also within the partner group. If the challenge of the programme would demand other skills or experiences as the programme progressed, the programme should let partners go and bring new ones in.

It is our experience that once you are engaged in a committed partnership, the incentives to radically change course, either in the activities, the resource allocation or the partner setup, decrease. We have experienced several times how partner contributions tend to draw on either the areas where the individual feels most professionally comfortable or where the organization has commercial or strategic interests. Often, partners are eager to stay in the projects for as long as possible due to vested interests – it is often in no one's interest to stand down, even if the value the partner creates is unclear.

With Decoupling 2030, the ambition was to create incentives that challenged the programme to *defy* these organizational interests that often drive many projects forward but do not necessarily directly address the root causes of the challenges they have set out to solve.

Decoupling 2030 is designed as an eight-year programme with loops of two-year portfolios. These portfolios consist of a series of *labs*, which are bespoke collaborations with groups of Danish manufacturing companies focusing on sustainable transition. These labs are flexible and targeted at the different barriers and opportunities for sustainable and circular transition. Every second year the portfolio is reviewed and evaluated, and, based on this evaluation, the coming portfolio will be planned and activities as well as partners may change.

The evaluation is conducted with both an internal and an external eye: an *insight group* of three people closely monitors, evaluates and facilitates strategic learning dialogue across the portfolio of labs with the partner groups. An external and independent *mission committee* of experts and researchers is involved every second year to examine the learnings and output from the insights group and relate these to the contextual developments within sustainability. As a result of this process, they will produce recommendations for the coming portfolio.

The strategic mandate to make decisions regarding the portfolio focus, funding allocation and the make-up of the partners is placed with the *mission board*. Importantly, the mission board is an independent group of individuals that have no active role in the programme and do not receive any organizational funding besides the fee they receive to carry out their work on the board. Their sole purpose and responsibility is to guide and steer the programme towards the long-term goal. This improves their ability and mandate to take unpopular decisions, for instance around resource allocation, partner group or strategic pivots.

'In Decoupling 2030 I have a place to go outside my own organization, where we can agree to set bold ambitious goals and we can be genuinely open and explorative about how to reach them in a way that is impossible within the confinements of our respective organizations', a partner in Decoupling 2030 told us.

In many ways the structure of Decoupling 2030 prepares the ground for power structures and decision making to be governed by the mission goal. In summary, this governance structure and portfolio model:

- Commits resources to ensure deep strategic learning (through the insight group).
- Creates structures and incentives to continuously adapt to the results of learning (the portfolio review).
- Ensures the qualification of portfolio learnings as well as bringing in new perspectives to challenge assumptions (through the mission committee).
- Leaves room for adaptation, replacement of partners, as well as structural pivots, as it guards against personal, organizational and commercial interest in driving the programme forward (through the mandate of the independent mission board).

As we write this book, the programme is approaching the first portfolio revision, preparing for evaluation and the first mission committee review. Therefore, it is too soon for us to pass judgement on the success of this model. There is no doubt that the governance model has been new to several of the people involved, and it has and continues to take time and energy for all partners to lean into these new and more flexible structures.

The role of the mission board, we have found, can be particularly demanding. A board, which typically functions as a unit to control and oversee operations and finance, is now urged to maintain a future-oriented and risk-willing approach – identifying and encouraging potential strategic turns and pivots. Since the goal of the programme is to mature new markets and build a new practice among Danish companies there is little best practice to lean on. This is a challenging situation to be in. And the uncertainty that fills the room of the board must be cushioned by insights, knowledge and support that steers the process forward. This is a tension that the programme must balance in a constructive way.

Backcasting: the speculative portfolio

As we uncovered in *Navigating a New Story*, we propose applying approaches from futures design to imagine and orchestrate a joint new direction for a given systemic challenge. Yet, we should not isolate our imaginative capabilities to solely focus on the far future. Our imagination is something we must continuously work on and to maintain as we unfold our portfolios. This is where we move into the very practical and cumbersome process of *backcasting*. Backcasting is a crucial element of futures design or transition design, which involves working backwards towards the present to identify the significant changes needed. It is an essential approach for turning a future vision into actionable steps.

In our conversations with researcher, innovator and entrepreneur within design, policy and transformation, Rowan Conway, she suggests that pathfinders need to apply a speculative approach to portfolios (Conway, 2024a). Conway exemplifies this through her work with the Royal Society of Chemistry and their mission to create sustainable polymers in liquid formulations (PLF). Here, the mission target for the global industry is to develop biodegradable PLFs and advance the circular economy infrastructure for these chemicals by 2030. The mission sets the course for a transition of the US$125 billion sector to become sustainable by 2040 (Royal Chemistry Society, 2023).

Over a nine-month period, as part of the Sustainable PLFs Task Force, Conway co-led a mission-driven design process with the goal to draw a 2040 innovation roadmap for sustainable PLF. The Royal Society of Chemistry was the anchor organization driving the task force forward, and to accommodate for the breadth and complexity of the challenge, the group invited in actors from across several domains. This larger group consisted of industry leaders from key sectors, experts from UK and European academia alongside national networks, UK funders and standards specialists.

In this process, Conway co-facilitated a process of answering the difficult question: 'What will it take for us to de-fossilize polymer chemicals?' Together they carried out a speculative portfolio exercise, conducting a systemic gap analysis that explored what would be required to move towards the 2040 vision. Thus, they identified which incentives would be needed to overcome the inherent barriers to change. The taskforce catalogued the different types of research, innovations, services and policy mixes that would constitute a speculative portfolio of system innovation, and they detailed the requisite roles needed from a range of actors such as policy makers, start-ups or scientists (Conway and Massey-Brooker, 2024).

Conway applied a speculative approach and worked consistently with the diverse group to develop the roadmap. Starting from the future vision, and from there assessing the steps towards implementation. The large idea of changing infrastructure and de-fossilizing chemicals was broken down into granular micro-experiments. This included zooming in on the everyday steps that had to be taken to undertake change. Over the course of the process, the goals and priorities of the roadmap were tested on different critical stakeholders in the industry to look for feedback as to whether the market was ready for the change. This process resulted in the development of several initiatives to mature the market, such as research consortia, developing proposals for joint research funding, and the establishment of a new centre for doctoral training focused on PLFs.

A mission-oriented approach that so radically insists that it is possible to overcome apparent structural barriers very quickly sparks resistance. Here, one micro-experiment Conway encouraged was for the group to reframe stakeholder communication around the challenge.

The default discourse in the task force was to put energy into arguing around the *why* of the problem, defending a mission-oriented approach for sustainable polymers to the people holding power in the industry. These barriers-focused arguments prolonged and slowed down the process. Conway therefore proposed shortcutting this focus and instead encouraged the group to reframe their dialogue through a new, more positive framing. This reframing of the problem challenged Royal Society of Chemistry employees to meet their stakeholders with a completely different approach, for example, starting a conversation like this: 'We are working to enable a step change in sustainable polymers; this experience may sometimes be different to your experience of innovation practices, and may feel uncomfortable – this is normal, and collaborative work will require that we get comfortable with being uncomfortable' (Conway, 2024a). Reframing a conversation may come off like a straightforward and harmless micro-experiment. Yet, Conway's experience was that this kind of change in behaviour and culture in a work environment can be downright nerve-wracking for professionals and senior staff who are used to a more safe, analytical and critical discourse. Put in our words, you might say they experienced the tension between the rational and the speculative mindset.

> Working with anticipatory prototyping means that you are exploring the road ahead before you walk it – this can be very uncomfortable because it can reveal the challenges ahead and show uncertainty. The biggest mindset shift is to help people moving into *possibility thinking* because when you are working with big sustainability transitions, and you start to do the detailed work, it can feel really overwhelming. Facilitating this process is an art, as the process of mapping the future might lead to big revelations about consequences that challenge assumptions behind supply chains or timelines. The designer needs to make space for absorption and reflection to help the participants comprehend that existing strategies may need rethinking. (Conway, 2024a)

In our opinion, Conway's work is both inspiring and thought-provoking because it reveals the granular practice of not just framing a mission but building a new practice for *possibility thinking* that persistently challenges our deeply entrenched institutional behaviour and the default rules, practices and knowledge systems of our everyday, modern life. The speculative portfolio approach is a strong example of how to juggle the balance between large goal setting with micro-experiments as well as nurturing both the speculative and the rational mindset.

Breaking down portfolios

We argue that portfolios should be broad, holistic, span across sectors and be 'spacious' enough to leave room for experimentation and failures. An obvious flipside here is that the broadness of mission portfolios increases the complexity and the scale of the work to such a degree that it will include everything and exclude nothing. It becomes insurmountable, unfocused and not impactful.

Portfolios must be broken down to be manageable. Fortunately, the goal of the mission can help us guide this analysis and prioritization.

Engholm uses the compelling image *systems acupuncture* to describe a targeted approach to systems change as 'models intended to soften systems and allow for new patterns to emerge' (Engholm, 2023). In planning and developing this portfolio, we look for the right, tense territories to stick in the needle, hoping to trigger new system dynamics. This demands a deep understanding of what drives the systems in the wrong direction or sustains the somewhat broken system and a curiosity about which drivers may pull behaviour, incentives, funding and structures in the right direction. The portfolio is not an end goal or an itinerary to slavishly follow. It is rather our compass to keep us on our toes regarding where to focus our efforts.

One structure that can help us guide the portfolio focus is the Three Horizon Framework, which we introduced earlier. It can serve as a strategic reference that may guide which *kind* of interventions we launch, helping us manage the varying temporalities of the transition. Roughly, the activities in the portfolio can be designed through this lens:

- Rehearsing the preferred future: Launching interventions and tests that are micro-versions or very early initial components of new solutions we want to test (this relates to Horizon 3).
- Enabling transition through temporal experiments: Temporal interventions and initiatives that allow for new perceptions, logics and structures to gain ground and to experience that things could be different. A kind of transmitter or catalyst. These experiments pave the way for other more permanent initiatives and more lasting solutions to emerge (this relates to Horizon 2).
- Composting experiments: Horizon 1 involves identifying things we must stop doing. It can be tough to discontinue

activities, processes, services or procedures that have shaped the system for many years. This horizon, therefore, involves exploring what happens when we no longer act traditionally and what new opportunities emerge in the absence of these old practices (as with the urine dipsticks).

A theory of change

To help us with the practical exercise of designing a mission portfolio that consists of different interventions that all relate to and affect the overall mission, we can backcast the goals of the preferred future into concrete stepping stones out of one system into another.

We recommend drawing on the Impact Framework for Mission-oriented Innovation developed by the Innovation Fund Denmark. This framework (see Figure 5.2) will help pathfinders set the portfolio's strategic focus and analyse the interdependence among portfolio projects, assessing whether they work in the same direction.

The framework helps the pathfinder analyse the different layers and connections in a mission portfolio, from the large and overarching challenge we set out to solve, to find the signs we

Figure 5.2: Innovation Fund Denmark's impact framework for mission-oriented innovation

Affected by external factors	Northern Star: The long-term goal of the mission
	Instances of impact
	Tipping points (inflection points)
Primarily within control of the mission	Enablers for change / Project portfolio
	Learning questions Milestones / Learning questions Milestones

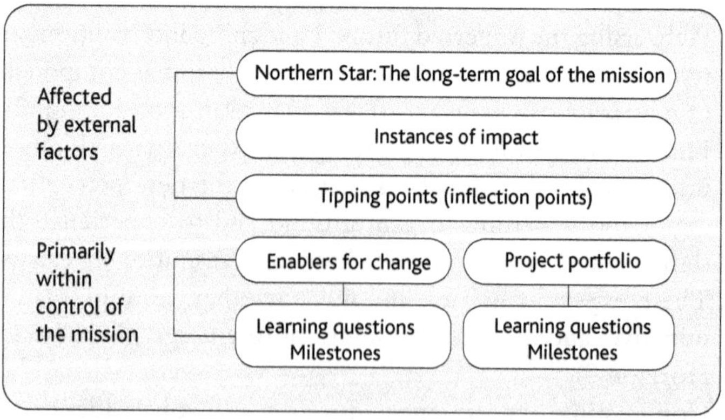

Source: Larsen et al (2024)

must look for, to understand better when and how that change happens. It helps us design targeted interventions and raise our awareness of what we are trying to learn.

A valuable aspect of this framework is that it helps us separate what lies *outside* and *inside* the influence of the mission and its portfolio.

Let us start with the top section, which includes elements outside the portfolio's direct control but deeply influence its implementation.

- *The North Star* marks the direction of the mission, the preferred future and the joint narrative we elaborated on in the first navigation point. It sets direction, builds momentum and is the reference point for all decisions.
- *Instances of impact* are the signs we may look for to monitor whether change is happening. As we work with long-term change, it may take several years before we witness the final effects of our efforts. Instead, we can look for smaller signs of change, such as small market shifts, new cultural behaviour, the maturing of new technology and positive market competition. These changes render the transition likely to happen instead of impossible.

As for *tipping points*, neither will a mission have complete control over these, but they may significantly influence them. Let us unpack what a tipping point is by using the example of electric cars:

- a *cultural* tipping point could be producing smart and attractive electric cars that appeal broadly to drivers and tie into a narrative and desirable personal brand and image;
- a *technological* tipping point could be the ability to produce batteries for electric cars with a sufficiently long range;
- a *market shift* tipping point could be producing batteries at such a low cost that they match fossil-fuelled cars;
- a *systemic* tipping point could be setting up charging stations broadly across the country;
- a *regulatory* tipping point might imply lowering the registration fee for electric cars.

These tipping points, combined, enabled a systemic shift in electric cars, which we are witnessing today. In 2024, electric cars were the preferred choice for Danes when buying a new car.

Two critical factors should determine which tipping points to focus on in a mission portfolio: (1) assessing which tipping points the mission is most likely to influence; and (2) understanding which tipping points are most pivotal for achieving the mission.

The bottom section of the framework constitute the mission's concrete *portfolio* of initiatives. Here, the framework guides you in choosing a focus for the portfolio that aligns with the selected tipping points and sets the direction for a wide range of projects. These focus areas are supported by milestones and learning questions that let the pathfinder monitor how the projects inform each other.

An element often overlooked and unsupported in portfolio work is the invisible fabric *around* the projects that enable them to succeed. This fabric concerns how people collaborate, contribute, learn, and share knowledge and resources to achieve the mission. In the framework, these elements are called *enablers of change*. These imply implementing transparent and inclusive governance models, mobilizing authentic engagement around the preferred future, enabling strategic learning across the partnership, building capacity for mission-oriented innovation and fostering multi-level collaboration.

Working with portfolios and theory of change and, thus, continuously refining our hypothesis on how we might create a valuable transition in the system calls upon us to be very vigilant to the fact that, in societal change processes, we are forever learning and adapting to results of our actions as well as to the effects of the changes in society around us. To act in this space, we must take an explorative mindset and get to know the nature and rules of the experiment, which plays the lead part in the upcoming navigation point, *Navigating Experiments*.

What we have learned so far: navigating balance

In *Navigating Balance*, we uncovered the inherent tension of opposing attitudes that dominate societal change. Pathfinders find themselves having to balance the continuous reciprocal interplay between different aspects of *time* (future versus present; long-term versus short-term), *scale* (large versus small; abstract versus concrete) and *mindset* (patient versus impatient; speculative versus rational). We stress that holding this tension is a condition for societal change processes.

Experience from the design practice gives us clues as to how to honour this tension. Through the designerly processes of moving between different stages of thinking and reasoning we can organize for these shifts in attitudes, zooming in and out of time, scale and mindset.

We identify an inclination towards the short-term in many places in our culture, societal structures and institutional practices today, therefore, we highlight the necessity of insisting on the long term in our narratives, our thinking, our planning and decision making.

We introduce mission-oriented innovation as a structure for framing our wicked societal challenges and our visions for how to solve them. We do this because missions accommodate the tension of opposing attitudes by focusing on the dynamic interplay between ambitious, long-term targets with bottom-up experimentation. Through emerging governance models, we may organize ourselves in new ways to solve complex problems.

Structuring our work through the mission portfolio helps us organize for and govern these complex change processes. It serves as a tool to start backcasting: breaking down the journey towards the ambitious North Star, the preferred future, into stepping stones from the now into the future. With a theory of change, we may target our interventions towards reaching the highest possible impact. And with a portfolio perspective we can keep a vigilant eye on how these different interventions are connected.

Navigating experiments

At a press conference on 11 March 2020, in the Hall of Mirrors at the Danish Prime Minister's Office, journalists are placed on every other chair as a visual echo of the virus spreading as a wildfire. The atmosphere is solemn and nervous as the prime minister enters the room and opens the meeting. The air feels heavy and thick, even for those of us watching the press conference live from our living rooms. Denmark is shutting down to contain the spread of COVID-19. The number of people infected with the virus has increased more than tenfold in just three days.

As the Danish prime minister talks us through the details and the carefully curated information on how to respond to the virus, she also states something quite unusual and unprecedented in the realm of political leadership:

> I would like to say to the entire Danish population that we are in uncharted territory in the situation we find ourselves in. We have not experienced this before. Will we make mistakes? Yes, we will. Will I make mistakes as prime minister? Yes, I will. And in many instances, we will also have to ask for patience. We cannot answer all the questions right now. (Prime Minister's Office, 2020)

Mette Frederiksen, the Danish prime minister, was not the only political leader to acknowledge the uncertainty and the need for swift action. In our interpretation this signalled a political resolve, a willingness to experiment, to learn and to adapt as our society's understanding of the accumulating crisis deepened. All over the world, political leaders came forward. In March 2020, Germany's Angela Merkel, New Zealand's Jacinda Ardern, Britain's Boris Johnson, Canada's Justin Trudeau and Norway's Jonas Gahr Støre reached the same conclusion and openly exposed their uncertainty to the public. Angela Merkel stated: 'We find ourselves in a situation that is serious and uncertain. We must act now, even though we do not have all the answers. We must act based on what we know, but also on what we do not know' (Raupp, 2022).

This very situation testified to a historic moment: political leaders showed a new kind of bravery and an unfamiliar vulnerability.

While the COVID-19 crisis led to many personally and economically devastating consequences, which, even five years later, are still developing, it showed how fast we can act with a different mindset. It is easy to start wondering – as many of us have done countless times: What would happen if this was the ethos with which we addressed the climate crises? That we do not have the full image and probably never will, but we need to start acting now based on what we know and what we do not know?

Navigating uncharted waters: acting without knowing all the answers

During the lockdown and the many following months of adjusted restrictions around socializing, it became the new normal to check the number of infected in your region and receive push notifications on your mobile screen, such as 'you have been close to someone who has been tested positive' and adapt accordingly to that information. The daily routine involved taking a COVID-19 test before we went to work.

We do not mean to ignore the resistance and local movements that criticized the political decisions made. Yet, we experienced an overriding societal consensus on the fact that we did not know the paths forward, that they were unclear. We may not have agreed on the different responses to the crisis, but there was a general acceptance within the public that we needed to experiment our way forward, learn and adapt to continuously uncover the next steps. As experimenting and learning from, for example, data and adapting to this became part of almost everyone's everyday routine, we cannot help but wonder: When the world is ever-changing, why can't we start experimenting with new approaches, paths and actions to navigate our way through the climate crisis, the mental health crisis among young people, the recruitment crisis, the refugee crisis, the democratic crisis and the inequality crisis? Are these crises not equally deep, far-reaching and if we look closer, urgent?

6

Untying the knot through experiments

In many cases the interwoven and intricate problems we refer to in this book are tied together so closely that we cannot find one end to start pulling in order to untie the, somewhat, Gordian knot. Even if we do, it might just tighten the knot and, to stay with the figurative speech, create new entanglements elsewhere.

At this point in the book, we have reached a third navigation point. We went through the importance of using our imagination to create new narratives and set a new shared direction to loosen the knot and see new paths in *Navigating a New Story*. Further, we have investigated another navigation point, *Navigating Balance*, describing the different attitudes and tensions we must embrace as pathfinders in order to skilfully discern which threads to pull. In this third navigation point, *Navigating Experiments*, we start intervening with the knot – pushing gently here, and pulling lightly there.

This navigation point is about experimenting to find new answers. Experiments – whether designed to make discoveries, test hypotheses or explore new possibilities – are vital for navigating societal transitions and for testing new methods and ideas.

As a pathfinder, being able to experiment entails a continuous openness, curiosity and responsiveness to the insights and developments that emerge during the course of actions.

Successfully embracing an experimental approach requires creativity, bravery and a shift in leadership style. Design's exploratory approach helps us activate this experimental mindset and build up our dynamic capabilities as leaders and in our respective organizations. We need these capabilities to challenge assumptions, navigate the unknown, ask curious questions and apply an empathetic mindset. Consequently, continuous learning and adaptation are essential parts of the everyday work of experimenting to navigate a societal transition.

The navigation point offers pathfinders a way to start experimenting and to take action while still exploring the problem and the challenge on a deeper level. We will take you through:

- How adopting an abductive mindset and a playful approach allows you to reframe norms and values, supporting another way of perceiving reality to discover new opportunities.
- How a safe psychological space is a prerequisite for wise experimentation.
- How to work in a hypothesis-driven way with experiments and adopt a learning forward approach, securing continuous adaptation and learning.
- How to adopt an experimental mindset, develop, broaden and anchor the learning practices in your organization, in partnerships and what new skills hinge on a reimagined leadership role.

Experiments as safeguards in the labyrinth of complexity

Analysing the COVID-19 situation underscores an essential point about how quickly we learn and progress if we experiment *together*. The COVID-19 case was presented as a state of emergency that forced us to come together to learn. What would happen if we transferred this learning mindset to a much broader array of the work that we carry out, obtaining a curious mindset about all the results, insights and learnings we gain from our many interactions with society?

Let us start by looking at what defines an experiment and what it means to experiment. We rely on the definition of an experiment as an operation carried out under controlled conditions in order to discover an unknown effect, to test or establish a hypothesis when following a standard procedure is not an option (Merriam Webster Dictionary, nd). Accordingly, when we initiate experiments, we send a probe into the world, we impact the world with an intervention, we learn from the outcomes, we adapt, we improve, and then do it again.

Talking about experiments often evokes reluctance. The word *experiment* carries the connotation that we do not entirely know where we will end up, that experiments are risky and uncontrollable – a form of gambling. It almost seems absurd to suggest that politicians should experiment, as they did in response to the COVID-19 crisis in 2020. That the highly skilled and experienced people we have elected do not have a well-structured and 'safe' plan to roll out in the time of crisis.

With that discourse as the backdrop, it is no surprise that throughout our career, we have met business leaders and top-level public sector managers who feel very uncomfortable with experimenting. Can 'strong' leaders acknowledge that they are paddling in unknown waters, uncertain about what the future brings?

Is it acceptable for a leader to doubt, to not know the answer, and to *try things out*? Does experimenting mean that political leaders are dodging their responsibilities? Would you support a head of state who experiments with our society and, hence, our lives and the lives of our children? This is uncharted territory, especially for political leaders expected to steer nations with a clear sense of direction.

We must meet these concerns and understand that the idea of experimenting may come across as a contradiction to our current paradigm of decision-making and planning. To some, the only thing the concept evokes is a tenacious scepticism. On several occasions, we have even omitted the word experiment, using words such as tests and trials to evade potential resistance.

We suggest responding to this scepticism by reasoning that experimenting, testing or trialling may be the only sound option when navigating unknown waters. Experimenting, when done right and adequately prepared, offers us a safe and more controlled approach to handling uncertainty, which, ultimately, helps us mitigate risks and systematically builds capacity in organizations for people to be ready to respond to change.

And, of course, experiments should never be carried out thoughtlessly but wisely and well-prepared. As Amy C. Edmondson, an inspiring researcher whose ideas and research we have been inspired by, suggests:

Intelligent failures begin with preparation. No scientist wants to waste time or materials on experiments that have been run before and failed. Do your homework. The classic intelligent failure is hypothesis driven. You've taken the time to think through what might happen – why you have reason to believe that you could be right about what will happen. (Edmondson, 2023: 23)

Experimenting towards the preferred future

When we advocate for building a new narrative around a preferred future in *Navigating a New Story*, we automatically embed a range of assumptions about this exact future. It is through experiments that we translate these assumptions into concrete actions from which we can learn about that preferred future.

Experiments are a powerful aid in balancing and embracing opposing attitudes, as described in *Navigating Balance*. Through experiments, we counterbalance the long-term narrative with something concrete, tangible and fast. A tangible experiment connects the patient and slow transition with the impatient need for short-term progression. It helps create small interventions that encourage and support your work, giving you concrete examples to communicate progress, and the feeling of moving towards something (slowly, yes, but moving though!) is palpable. It creates agency. In that sense, experiments serve as a binder between the opposite attitudes adding weights to the scales.

There are several skills we need to train and acquire when experimenting and learning to bridge the more traditional way of approaching problems with new ones. Let us scrutinize these in the coming sections.

The cognitive leap

Policymakers and practitioners are largely unready for the shift in practice that needs to take place to support long-term transformative innovation and sustainability efforts on the scale that the climate crisis demands. Design offers a way to cross the 'say-do-gap' with wise experimentation. (Conway, 2024b)

In 2020, a Danish government agency asked the Danish Design Center (DDC) to facilitate a dialogue at a theme day for 140 employees from different offices and domains. They wanted to broaden their awareness of the future society and, in turn, their future role as a public agency: their interactions, the potential interfaces and the logics and dynamics that could emerge. In their perspective the ability to orient themselves toward longer-term perspectives and consider multiple futures and developments simultaneously was lacking or non-existent. They had an increasing sense that the right skills, which would be required in the near future, were not well-developed or even entirely missing within the organization. They wanted to spark new ideas and advancements to prepare for the future.

The government agency was interested in utilizing the DDC's previous work on future scenarios, *Living Futures*. *Living Futures* is an evocative listening experience, and a toolkit built around four alternative futures set in the year 2050, providing an exploratory space for people to understand, discuss and shape the future together (DDC, 2020).

A selected group of employees from DDC conducted an interactive, playful and exploratory session with the agency's staff, ranging from top level management and long-time employed experts to newly qualified administrative officers and student assistants. The session avoided lengthy presentations and endless slideshows, opting instead for a more hands-on involvement with audio files, images and tangible artefacts representing the alternative futures.

Several participants hesitated and felt uncomfortable. Some even resisted and rejected it as frivolous. However, after some time, as a few people began to play along, the hesitant ones found the courage to take it seriously, surrender to their imagination and lean into exploration on their own. It ultimately became an uplifting, creative and empowering experience.

The feedback afterwards was that the session had truly sparked a dialogue across domains and hierarchy that continued not just the next day or weeks but became a shared central experience serving as a reference point in their everyday work in solving different tasks and pursuing new tracks in the organization.

In addition to divergent and convergent approaches in design, *abductive reasoning* is an essential ingredient to the designerly way of working with systems change. Much of the economic and political thinking that has primarily formed our society today is founded on deductive and inductive thinking: deductive thinking draws on historical data from existing theories, and inductive reasoning is based on probability from empirical findings.

Yet, we need alternative ways of reasoning for us to take what Conway calls *the cognitive leap*: to be able to introduce alternative pathways to a more sustainable future. And, as we highlighted in *Navigating a New Story*, to build our imaginative skills for new and better problem solving. This is where abductive reasoning is helpful. It refers to the process of value creation through problem-solving by creating space for ideation, experimentation and creativity (Dorst, 2011). Abductive reasoning is, in our perspective, a premise to experiment, as abduction is a form of qualified or educated guesswork driven by our hypotheses (Engholm, 2023).

As Engholm puts it, abductive reasoning is a way of 'navigating the unknown and working with problems and solutions in an interactive process'. Thus, we take it seriously that many innovative solutions and ideas do not arise from analytic, linear and prescriptive reasoning. We also acknowledge that novel insights and new value can best arise if we are open to a more exploratory, iterative and sensory way of thinking and working.

According to Engholm, abduction is the crucial moment in the design process because it is the moment in which ideas or hypotheses are generated. It is a thinking move that springs from such impulses as 'What if?' or 'Might it be that …?' (Engholm, 2023).

The example of Boxing Future Health and Vorby we walked through in *Navigating a New Story* and the latter case with the Danish government agency are examples of how design processes stimulate abductive reasoning that challenges our, sometimes delimited, outlook. What if the future of healthcare was something completely different? Here, the sensory experience of tangibly visiting an alternative future stimulates new connections and ideas within the participant – to think outside the borders of one's profession, mandate, task or even the system as we know it. To look for new possibilities and to dare to let oneself play along in a safe, exploratory space.

When we recall images of the engaged crowd of civil servants from the Danish government agency and the large room, buzzing with life, excitement and curiosity where people exchange smiles across the room, even bursting out in laughter and enthusiastically debating and arguing seriously about a completely different role of the public agency, it reveals a significant clue to an essential ingredient that stimulates abductive reasoning: the power of playfulness.

Staying serious yet playful

> Why is a slide deck, meeting, or spread sheet considered more serious than a game, performance, or short story? (Østergaard, 2024b)

A few years ago, in the process of revisiting and reframing the DDC's strategy, we reflected upon our past years' work. A colleague pinpointed something interesting, as he said: 'In a way we managed to stay deeply serious, but yet playful in our work.' As those were two opposing positions to take.

His conception was, however, not spun out of thin air. It was a familiar feeling many of us had experienced during our careers: you cannot be both serious with important and major challenges, hold real power and have influence if you insist on being playful and explorative. Coming from the creative field of design, we have both learned to walk this fine line because we believed in and saw the massive value of a creative, playful and explorative mindset but persistently wanted to be taken seriously and influence the 'real deal'.

As you move into your role as a pathfinder and you start thinking differently about your challenge, you might feel the same way. Can I be deeply serious about my cause and still create space for creativity, playfulness and curiosity?

We have both felt this way on more occasions than we can count. And even, to be honest, writing this book, we discussed many times how we can be taken seriously by the broad system of civil servants, policy makers, private companies, philanthropic organizations and investors when we propose to imagine and dream about a different future as a vital tool to impact the world's serious challenges.

The struggle is real, even for hard believing pioneers.

Nevertheless, we insist on embracing being both playful and serious. We can hold both at the same time, and they actually go hand in hand.

'If adult life contains no play, because we feel too uncomfortable or silly, our ability to generate new thoughts and make new connections depletes' Rob Hopkins says (Hopkins, 2019). Following Hopkins' perspectives, the question becomes what might happen if play was a recognized tool that was used in politics, in leadership, in everyday life? Integrated and cultivated. What new connections and thoughts would appear, or, as Hopkins asks: 'Would it decrease anxiety? Would it build empathy? Would it establish connections? (Hopkins, 2019).

We can look back in history to the Dutch historian Johan Huizinga, a founding father of cultural history, who served as inspiration for many studies within sociology and anthropology; he addresses with his book, *Homo Ludens* from 1931, the profound importance of play for our society to evolve and flourish. He argues convincingly that the human being is a creature whose nature is to create and participate in play: 'For many years, the conviction has grown upon me that civilisation arises and unfolds in and as play' (Huizinga, 1938).

If it is in our nature already, then perhaps it is more of a question of reconnecting with it? If we dig a bit deeper to understand the notion of playfulness, literature introduces *playful seriousness* as an attitude that enables us to approach tasks and responsibilities with a light-hearted, creative and imaginative perspective that renders motivation, openness and engagement (The Fifth Dimension, 2023). It empowers more people to engage and interact, as play can break through our norms and allow communication through means other than the spoken word, such as written long reports and slide decks. You might argue that play becomes a language available and accessible to the many instead of the few.

Turning to the reversed concept of *serious playfulness* it refers to taking leisure activities, hobbies and pastimes seriously with the intent to learn and grow. Serious playfulness allows us to express ourselves through other means and ways, but with a focused, intentional attitude.

The Dutch researcher and professor Joost Vervoort from Transformative Imagination at Utrecht University suggests that 'deep seriousness and deep playfulness are not opposites, but very closely related' (Vervoort, 2022). He adds that playfulness can help loosen the constraints of society and its values and, thereby, support another way of perceiving and accepting reality. It can redefine what is considered natural and acceptable and challenge existing power structures and philosophies. In other words, playfulness sparks imagination around new societal alternatives.

When we're playful, we are wilfully not taking things as they are, not accepting their normal interpretations. Playfulness can be another path into the depth, mystery and complexity of life, with an emphasis on its absurdity and ironic hilarity. It also points to endless possibilities for imagining things otherwise (Vervoort, 2022).

Deep seriousness and deep playfulness address the complexity and depth of human activities that might not be immediately apparent yet are crucial for understanding the cultural and social fabric of a community (see Figure 6.1). These attitudes help us move beyond the superficial act of 'scratching the surface'. Without it, there is a risk that we continue *sleepwalking*, as Vervoort calls it, following conventions, common ideas and expected behaviours, failing to engage deeply with our surroundings. Consequently, there is a risk that we will miss out on engaging in change.

A playful discovery

The scene is set, and you step into a glimpse of something unknown yet familiar. You are surrounded by a sense that this *is* indeed another world. The room is dark but filled with other faces illuminated by the soft orange light from the fire. The atmosphere is earnest and eager.

You do not doubt, you do not falter. It is a game. But we take the game deeply seriously. There is a mutual consensus among the 60 participants: We are here to explore and work with what our world would look like, how we go to work, how we fall in love, how we play sports, how we share a meal – even how play is an entirely integrated part of our everyday life. This city is built on entirely different principles. It is built on the principle that the well-being of humans, species and nature is the purpose of our society.

In the city you have stepped into, play and imagination is essential. It cultivates the city council to play and draw when making decisions about the city's expansion for housing, the construction of a new algae farm or the erection of a new school.

It is a wonderful place, but it is no utopia. In the dark during the annual Night Festival, you explore and celebrate the solace, community and the beauty of the night.

The scene is from an event at an international conference on the well-being economy in Copenhagen in 2024. The purpose was to create a tangible, bodily experience and sketch out, through play,

Figure 6.1: Deep seriousness versus deep playfulness

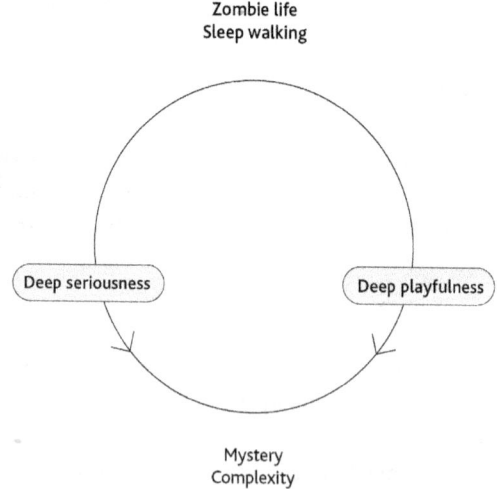

Source: Vervoort (2022)

Untying the knot through experiments

what the future could look like if we dare to challenge existing logics, paces, horizons and purposes and place an otherwise abstract concept like well-being in the centre of it.

The participants were moved and heartened when we all returned outside the dark room and back to reality. We asked them to reflect upon the experience and let them backcast and point out small pockets of opportunities, such as small glimpses of change that are already present today and can be explored and enlarged. Their response was overwhelming to us. It was evident that the immersive experience had left a significant mark on them as human beings, not just conference guests.

Circling back to our own reluctance and at times hesitation around playfulness: In times like that we remember that indeed you can, in fact you must, be both serious and playful when searching for new pathways in the wilderness of complex problems. That thought can be useful to revisit from time to time, when you experience doubt or resistance in your own mind or in your relationship with others.

When we experiment, we play.
When we experiment, we look for new answers.

Dare to question

It requires a certain level of safety and trust to dare step forward. To experiment, take chances and follow your gut. To ask the curious questions that hold no immediate answer. And to express wonder and appear hopeful, which may come off as being naive. This requires psychological safety.

Edmondson introduces psychological safety as: 'The belief that one will not be punished or humiliated for speaking up with ideas, questions, concerns, or mistakes and that the team is safe for interpersonal risk-taking' (Edmondson, 1999: 354).

She suggests that:

> For knowledge work to flourish, the workplace must be one where people feel able to share their knowledge! This means sharing concerns, questions, mistakes, and half-formed ideas. In most workplaces today, people are holding back far too often – reluctant

to say or ask something that might somehow make them look bad. (Edmondson, 2018: 22)

Psychological safety is an essential precondition for working with societal transitions across domains, professions, organizations and hierarchies. Questioning, experimenting and playing are fostered through safety. Try to recall our example from the government agency: the initial hesitation and the resistance. As soon as a few of the participants leaned in and showed that they dared to be playful, curious and vulnerable, the more hesitant ones gave in and joined the game as well.

Societal transitions will require making choices and sacrifices. We have mentioned this before. It involves disagreements, resistance and negotiations. Therefore, nurturing and fostering psychological safety is also crucial during challenging times as a pathfinder.

'Removing your mask helps others remove theirs. Of course, this means acting as if you feel psychologically safe, even if you might not be fully there yet. Sometimes, you have to take an interpersonal risk to lower interpersonal risk', Edmonson establishes (2018: 200).

7

Learning through hypothesis

The process of learning is a dynamic interplay between a hypothesis and the concrete interventions you put into the world. Whatever its scope, scale, purpose or context, an experiment consists of three elements that interact in loops:

- The hypothesis frames the assumptions you have around a given challenge or opportunity.
- The intervention is the concrete action you set in place to test and learn whether your assumptions are right or wrong.
- The learning describes the insights you gain from the intervention that triggers new and more qualified hypotheses to be tested through new interventions (thus, a new loop starts).

Hypotheses are what drive experiments and learning and, therefore, enable us to navigate the unknown. A hypothesis is a preliminary explanation or a qualified guess, based on observations, existing knowledge or theories. Hence, your hypotheses are the specific assumptions, ideas and hunches that define how you approach a process. They describe what you think you know, but do not fully know or do not know enough about yet.

When creating your hypothesis, we stress that you, as a pathfinder, need to direct your awareness towards the preferred future that guides your transition process. And then towards the unknowns of this preferred future. In practice, this means collecting all the questions you are trying to answer, being aware of what you know, what you think you know, and what you are unsure of. Make sure to be critical towards your own answers and analysis. Building this expanded consciousness about the unknown and the unknown unknowns can help guide experimentation.

Defining and testing your hypotheses in experiments is not just an introductory exercise. It is ongoing and must be repeated several times throughout the process in a systematic way, as learning condenses. We continually grasp, collect and respond to the learning. We build a learning practice.

Reducing loneliness among young students in Norway

Let us explore how working with hypotheses and experiments takes shape in practice through an example from Norway carried out by the Oslo-based design agency, Comte Bureau.

Comte Bureau initiated a collaboration with SIT, the Norwegian Student Welfare Organization, an organization that provides student housing, healthcare and recreational activities to student residents in Norway. Together, they set out with the ambition to reduce loneliness among students. The collaboration was co-led by architect Joana Sá Lima and Adrian Hasnaoui Haugen from Comte Bureau involving a team of service designers, psychologists, anthropologists and architects.

In a post-COVID-19 environment, awareness was rising of the severe consequences of a growing loneliness in the Norwegian population – especially among young people. Research and informal observations indicated increased levels of loneliness, specifically among university students living in physical campus environments lacking opportunities for social interaction.

The collaboration between the two parties was driven by several hypotheses that touched upon both spatial and social aspects of loneliness:

- Loneliness results from physical isolation and lack of connection with one's living environment.
- Shared spaces in student housing can reduce loneliness by facilitating spontaneous social interactions.
- When students perceive shared spaces as *their own*, they will use them and form connections with their peers.

These assumptions were based on data, professional experience and qualitative dialogues with students.

Thus, the overall focus and framing of the project became: 'How might architectural design reduce student loneliness by enhancing communal spaces and fostering social interaction?' (Lima, 2024).

We will get back to how they approached the hypothesis later. First, we need a short introduction to the concept of prototyping.

Prototyping as a learning vehicle

To test your hypothesis through interventions and experiments, we can turn to a well-known methodology from product design: *prototyping*. Through prototyping, designers develop tangible physical models of an idea to test and qualify different aspects of a new solution. In the early stages, prototypes can test whether the concept – the potential new product – is valuable to its user.

For example, in the context of a hospital, prototypes could be a visual sketch or a quick mock-up of a new surgical instrument so that users (the doctor or nurse) can more immediately relate to its relevance and value. Later in an innovation process, more high-fidelity prototypes can test functionality. Here, prototypes may test, for example, how a needle moves through the tissue. But the prototype can also test how a product interacts with and influences a work procedure, for example, how does the surgeon and the nurse interact with the instrument? What work processes are alternated and challenged with the use of the instrument?

Through the past 30 years, as the physical world has become more and more integrated with the digital world, prototyping is no longer only bound to give shape to physical products but also to digital products, services and even processes. Ergo, prototyping can be graphical illustrations, virtual models, spaces and enactments (Bason, 2010). As Bason points out, prototypes also serve as a means for collaboration and mutual understanding across professionals: 'A key strength of prototypes is that they allow for common understanding and dialogue about a proposed solution not only across internal disciplines and hierarchies but also between the "system" and the "users"' (Bason, 2010: 197).

We suggest expanding the notion of prototyping even further when applying it for systems change. Prototypes are used not only to qualify concepts, functionality and a shared understanding of new solutions. They can be applied as a vehicle for learning about the problem. As you work to find a new path forward and loose and undo the knot, you can use prototypes to test your hypothesis and deepen your learning about the challenge you are facing long before thinking about concrete solutions. In that sense prototypes serve as learning interventions that drive progress and movement forward.

Let us return to the work of reducing loneliness among students in Norway. To gather solid input for their hypotheses, the team carried out an in-depth prototyping phase through a series of workshops and 1:1 spatial simulations involving 100 students and staff. A 300m^2 room was prepared, simulating a section of a lobby for a potential student building. Here participants used elements like movable walls, cardboard boxes and furniture to recreate spatial layouts.

Comte Bureau facilitated three simulations: In the first simulation, participants designed the space collaboratively, building their own ideal community by placing programmes and activities while discussing their reasoning. In the second round of simulations, the focus was on specific spatial arrangements, such as how the laundry area interacted with other functions and areas. Participants placed furniture and elements to explore functional relationships. For the final round of simulations, the emphasis shifted to movement flow and interactions. Participants worked together to map how people would navigate the space.

These simulations helped the team better understand both the problem and its opportunities, which enriched their initial hypothesis around loneliness, physical space, and social interaction. Some of the key findings were that placing central functions – like laundry rooms – at the heart of shared spaces encouraged social engagement, as students naturally congregated in these areas. The absence of constant institutional supervision and the use of booking systems were also highlighted as crucial for creating a welcoming atmosphere where students could take ownership of the space without feeling overly monitored.

Moreover, students responded positively to spaces they could customize, reinforcing the hypothesis that a sense of ownership increases engagement and connection. Movable furniture and flexible layouts were key factors in making communal areas inviting and comfortable.

The insights gathered from the workshops and simulations were directly applied to the final design recommendations for the physical design of the student housing building Nardovegen 12–14. And while the project is still under construction, the model, process and tools developed during this initiative are already being implemented in other building projects.

The way Comte Bureau worked through prototyping gave a deep understanding of the needs of students: observations, interventions and workshops around the physical simulation provided the team with rich insights into the students' challenges, particularly loneliness and social isolation.

When we sat down with Joana for a chat in the spring of 2024, she highlighted how the project 'embodied a human-centred approach to architecture, where spaces are not just physical environments but tools that can address societal issues. In this case, it meant designing spaces, activities, services and a process that fosters a sense of belonging, community, and well-being – shaping the future of student housing' (Lima, 2024). The experiences from Comte Bureau lets us zoom in and understand the power of the experiment, of the dynamic interplay between hypothesis, intervention and learning in practice.

Now, let us step back and zoom out again.

We can address our work with societal change as a *portfolio of experiments* (Striegler et al, 2023). The experiments within the portfolio contribute to understanding the nature of the problem and the challenge as they are enacted in the real world. Hence, the experiments move us through our emerging learning from the experiments, slowly and over time, closer to the preferred future.

Recognizing this dynamic of how learning becomes the connector of experiments and what drives us forward necessitates an investment in learning, particularly collective learning across the portfolio. We want to continuously learn while staying alert, intercepting the signals to understand when it might be necessary to mobilize additional stakeholders, establish completely new experiments or even shut down futile initiatives.

Learning forward

> In an explorative process, we can move through various fields of possibility, stop to examine a given space without a set goal in mind and suddenly notice a new possibility. The precondition for making such serendipitous finds is that we learn to both dwell in open spaces of possibility and to use the input, data, and stimuli that we stumble upon. (Engholm, 2023: 100)

Learning happens in a constant loop but also at different paces. As Engholm points out, learning can even occur on the side of what you expected and initially set out for. This means that, as we build structures around our work to facilitate a constant orientation towards learning, we must remain vigilant that learning can surprise us and plan for flexibility to adapt to new insights.

One of us attended an event on democracy, where a civil servant from one of the largest Danish municipalities made the following confession: 'We spend 99.9 per cent of our time budgeting. While we carefully monitor whether the numbers balance, it is striking how little time we use to observe the outcome and results of what we put out into the world.'

While we admire her honesty, this is an alarming statement. It is striking how many resources the majority of organizations today put into planning and monitoring and how little they put into learning and assessing impact.

As Professor of Communication and Psychology David Budzt Pedersen briskly puts it, 'knowledge does not travel by itself'. In fact, if we do not proactively capture knowledge and transform it into learning, it remains inaccessible. It is stored in our minds and dissolves into thin air as projects end, and people change jobs or retire. Therefore, our obligation as pathfinders, when operating in the realm of uncertainty, is to harvest and share learning and respond to it through new actions.

Consequently, learning is something we must invest in. And we are confident that resources can be balanced by toning down energy and time spent on meticulous planning, short-term budgeting, reporting, monitoring and documentation processes. Instead, we can dedicate resources to learning from the interventions we put into the world and the many inputs around us. Learning is a core practice if we want to make a real impact. We must develop a culture, processes and mechanisms that continually enable us to sense and learn – not only because of the constant change and ambiguity that requires experimentation but also because there is already a wealth of knowledge that we could be using much more effectively. We need to operate as what we call a *learning organism*.

Learning at different scales

As explained in *Navigating Balance*, in systems change, we are obliged to manoeuvre and operate on different scales simultaneously: addressing the large problem but through constant, small and iterative actions. Accordingly, we must *learn* at various scales. Make sure that we harvest learnings from our small experiments and relate these to learnings across the portfolio to impact the challenge.

The model shown in Figure 7.1 illustrates these different levels of learning on a scale from micro to macro, recognizing that all levels inform each other. To stay with the previous metaphor of the entangled knot, we suggest that a heightened awareness of learning across the portfolio strengthens our ability to understand the challenge and how to decide on the next steps forward: As we pull the thread and communicate what we learn, we might discover where to pull next, or where to pull harder or more gently.

The model shown in Figure 7.1 increases our awareness of which type of learning to pick up on different levels. We suggest using this model as a backdrop for how to organize learning into your governance model and organizational processes that fit your specific context. We encourage you to design activities into your schedule or project plan with the specific aim, timing and context for people to adapt to this learning. It can be as part of

Figure 7.1: Harvesting Learning Model

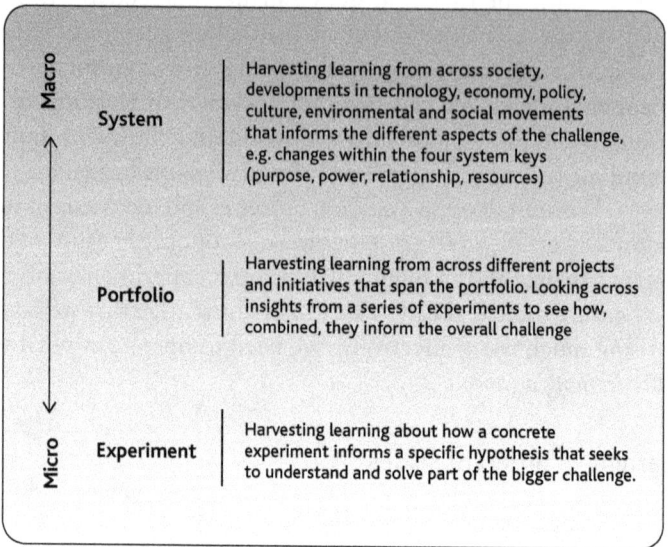

team, advisory, steering group or board meetings. The purpose is to carve out time and space for a group to harvest learnings and to adapt these into subsequent activities and plans. A necessary circumstance for this adaptation is for programmes and projects to be initially designed with flexibility, to cultivate a readiness in making continuous adjustments and changes.

Transitioning from foster care to adulthood

To describe how learning on different scales works in practice, we introduce an example from a societal challenge around foster care and placements in Denmark.

The transition from foster care to adulthood is a highly vulnerable and complex process for the young individuals involved. Along with their newly gained authority, young people in foster care who turn 18 also transition into a different administrative affiliation. This is a transition that causes a significant change in the public support they have previously received. Often these at-risk youths find themselves completely alone, deprived of the support that many of their peers take for granted. Studies show that this lack of both relational and practical support frequently pushes them to the margins of society, where they struggle without access to employment, education, stable housing or a social network.

The Danish mission-driven philanthropy, Bikuben Foundation, is dedicated to supporting *young people on the edge*. For many years we have been working closely with the foundation, exploring and experimenting with new approaches in their philanthropic means and initiatives. As part of one of their missions, *a safe passage and transition from care to adulthood*, the foundation has put forward an innovation capacity programme called Innovation Process for Placements to learn more about this exposed group and to reframe and develop new support structures. We sat down with Jakob Schjørring, Director of Social Affairs at the Bikuben Foundation, to gain insight into his perspectives and experiences – shaped over years of working not just on this youth mission, but in his and the foundation's broader role as a philanthropic enabler. Schjørring emphasizes that the foundation's role is to support and create spaces where radical ideas can emerge, breathe and be put into play. He shared a wise reflection: 'There will always be things you cannot answer when working with radical new ideas. It is simply in their nature: they often challenge the status quo and will frequently lack many answers. Therefore, radical ideas are easy to dismiss, and as a result, they are rarely explored' (Schjørring, 2025). Schjørring advocates for developing hypotheses to bridge and help translate our radical visions and dreams about creating change into something tangible we can test actively and concretely in a real-life setting.

Working with a hypothesis-driven approach requires a different mindset because structured learning becomes more than nice-to-have. It becomes a formal key performance indicator (KPI). It is not about whether the idea has succeeded. For this reason, experiments that fail are equally important for influencing and advancing an agenda.

> As a foundation, we initially thought that if we just invested in innovation sandboxes allowing people to experiment, they would be excited to dive into testing all sorts of ideas. But it turned out that it was

too challenging without a clear guiding star, leading to confusion and frustration among our partners. Everyone, including our partners, needs to know when they are doing well. When are we a success? We have now learned that to get the most out of the hypothesis-driven approach, we need to support our partners in establishing and maintaining a very clear vision for a preferred future. A preferred future that they can then explore through several experiments. With this point of departure, success is when a particular experiment has created new knowledge about the potential of their preferred future and how we might realize that potential in the best possible way. (Schjørring, 2025)

When writing this book, one of the many initiatives in the foundation's mission portfolio was the innovation capacity programme put forward with a strong emphasis on being hypothesis-driven, learning-oriented and fuelled by experiments. The programme involved three different projects and, hence, three different project teams.

Each project team was formed by a partnership across a municipality and a non-governmental organization with support from the foundation's social team. They focus on the following three questions as part of the overall mission theme, which is to create a safe passage and transition from foster care to adult life:

- How might we increase the likelihood that young people's existing resources and relationships will accompany them throughout the transition?
- How might the transition support and acknowledge young people's potential and make them feel important to others?
- How might we create a more needs-based choice of accommodation for young people?

The questions emerged from the engagement of former and current young people in foster care, carried out by De Anbragtes Vilkår, an advocacy organization founded by former children in placement and foster care.

Through observation, user insights and expert knowledge, each project team formulated hypotheses and translated them into *learning questions*. This process led them to analyse what they thought they knew and what they were unsure of about the hypotheses. It helped them structure their learning questions and equipped them to observe the linkages and dependencies across the different hypotheses. The work enabled them to structure their efforts and determine where to begin. Then, they began to design and initiate experiments that could further deepen their understanding of the hypotheses.

Let us take a deeper look at how one of the teams conducted their learning process through the lens of the three scales from Figure 7.1: experiment, portfolio and system.

Harvesting learning from experiments

The team's overarching hypothesis was that young people in foster care and young people living with their families, that is, those not in foster care, can be a resource for each other in the situation that all young people face at some point in their lives: moving out of their homes, having to support themselves, and standing on their own feet. The hypothesis was that this common specific life situation could create a shared third space for young people to connect, independent of their mixed backgrounds.

Returning to Schjørring's point that radical ideas often struggle to survive in their early stages without the right conditions, the foundation tested this idea and hypothesis with experts and stakeholders and received several critical questions. While the feedback revealed an immediate resistance to the idea, dismissing it would have been the easy choice. But rather than letting unanswered questions bring it to an end, they chose a different path: committing the team to explore some of these critical questions through a series of experiments.

The team initiated a series of experiments to gain insights into the hypothesis. They created a series of sub-hypotheses to further nuance their central hypothesis. And then they started their experimentation from the sub-hypotheses, translating them into micro-experiments. Their learning objective was to understand the following, as a prompting question for their sub-hypothesis: What is needed to ensure that both youth not in foster care and youth in foster care are willing to participate in common youth groups? How can they be mutually meaningful and equally significant to each other?

A concrete example from the team's work with micro-experiments was exploring various life situations and experiences that momentarily foster a sense of community among young people, without considering background or life circumstances. For instance, they initiated and observed what happens when a group of young people (both those in care and those not in care) upcycle second-hand furniture. Here, the team explored what is needed and what dynamics might emerge when young people individually and collectively experience a sense of being meaningful to others within this kind of temporal micro-community taking shape.

Another micro-experiment involved bringing together people who were once part of the target group but are now adults – those who had been in care and those who had not – to discuss their circumstances, challenges, needs and knowledge during the transition from youth to adulthood and the process of finding a home. The aim was to extract learnings from their experiences to inform the next generation (see the breakdown of the hypothesis and experiments visualized in Figure 7.2).

The team tested different approaches and harvested the learnings through bi-weekly learning meetings, using a digital platform to collect their insights, serving as a kind of 'learning bank'. This was no easy task, requiring the team members to resist the urge to see the experiments not as versions of a future solution but as vehicles for learning. They also had to avoid the inherent impulse to document their learnings in lengthy written detail.

The team structured their learning repository using digital note boards, which represented the overarching hypotheses and learning questions, the underlying sub-hypotheses, sub-goals and the experiments. The note board served as a tool for the bi-weekly meetings across the non-governmental organization and the municipality. The idea was that it could help them focus on shared learning, both in terms of how insights from the various experiments fed into new experiments and sub-goals and in relation to the larger overarching strategic learning objectives.

Learning through hypothesis

Figure 7.2: Breaking down the learnings: from foster care to adulthood

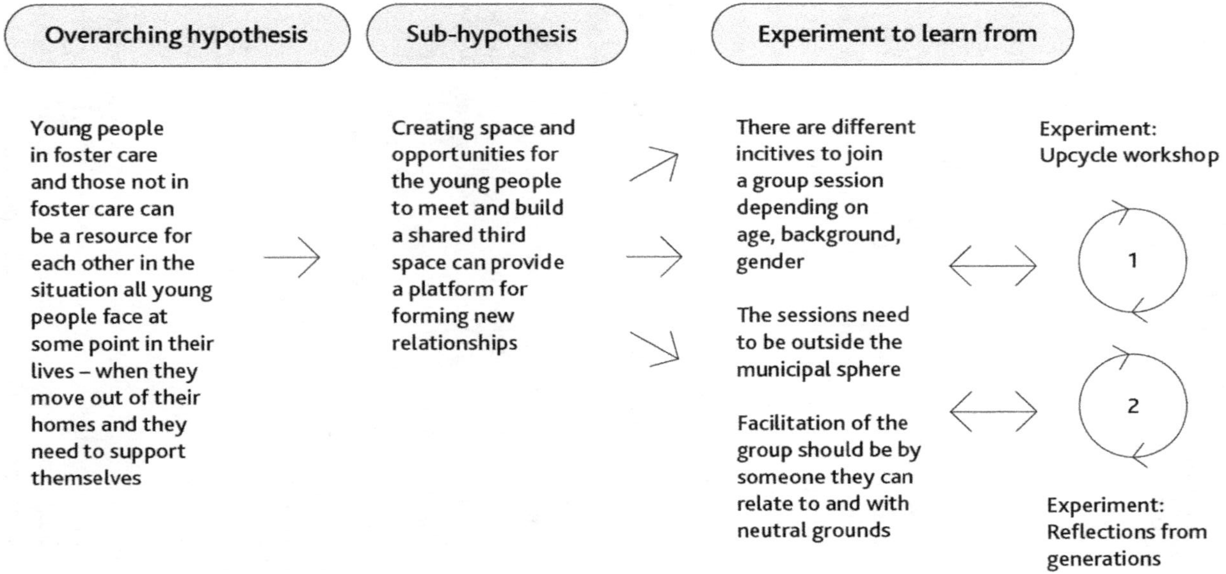

Overarching hypothesis	Sub-hypothesis	Experiment to learn from	
Young people in foster care and those not in foster care can be a resource for each other in the situation all young people face at some point in their lives – when they move out of their homes and they need to support themselves	Creating space and opportunities for the young people to meet and build a shared third space can provide a platform for forming new relationships	There are different incitives to join a group session depending on age, background, gender	Experiment: Upcycle workshop ↻ 1
		The sessions need to be outside the municipal sphere	
		Facilitation of the group should be by someone they can relate to and with neutral grounds	Experiment: Reflections from generations ↻ 2

Instead of writing detailed reports on their learnings, these learning meetings became quite central: the learning expanded, sharp and condensed insights were recorded in the repository, and new knowledge fed into new experiments.

Harvesting learning across the portfolio

The three teams had several hypotheses and learning points, which, together, gave them an indication of how they could address the overarching question: How might we create a more needs-based choice of housing for young people? And how might the transition support and acknowledge the potential of the young people in foster care and make them feel important to others?

As the programme's overall aim was to address the systemic problem of the transition from foster care and placement to adulthood, the three different project teams approached the problem and the questions from various angles within their local context. This did not mean cross-learning was irrelevant among the three teams and projects. The learnings inspired and provided shortcuts to knowledge in terms of both process and content for the teams.

Each of their many experiments, woven together, shaped other initiatives beyond the programme's boundaries – offering concrete input to the Bikuben Foundation's Policy Lab. When writing the book, the foundation was preparing a new cycle of work, transforming several policy recommendations into tangible action areas. The idea is that the insights and experiences cultivated by the three teams will flow into the broader portfolio. In this way, their work becomes the first stepping stone, guiding the next wave of experiments and interventions.

System level learning

The learnings and insights that naturally arose across the teams, and the many hypotheses, were relevant for influencing the national level, including policies, legislation and regulatory guidelines. Specifically, the foundation helped capture insights and bring them into play with decision-makers through policy labs, conferences, roundtables and op-eds. During the course of the programme, a new law, the Child's Law, was enacted and adopted. It focuses on extending support beyond the age of 18, individualized strategies and support processes, increased involvement of the youth, and emphasized enduring relationships. The Child's Law recognized that stable housing is a crucial prerequisite for a successful transition to adulthood. Therefore, the law includes mechanisms to ensure that young people from the foster care system do not find themselves without a safe place to live once they reach adulthood.

In some cases, external events affect the portfolio and programme and the experiments to such an extent that projects may need to slow or shut down. In this case, the new law could act as wind in the sails for the three teams. The political attention and demand made their work highly relevant and legitimate. This opened an even greater opportunity to utilize the specific learnings from their experiments to impact and deliver concrete and tested solutions in response to demands from the political level. However, it required them to connect the dots and link their experiments and learnings to both strategic and political levels. The effects of this process remain to be analysed after writing this.

Measuring the impact

A dominant driver of how we learn today is our monitoring and evaluation structures. Today, several organizations report on deliverables and KPIs that do not necessarily align with what we want to learn about. In fact, strict performance goals might even derail us from learning, as we may become more focused on 'ticking the boxes' in our reporting schemes than on learning whether the activity actually worked in the intended – or a surprisingly unintended – way. So, if we need to fundamentally change how we learn and adapt to insights, we must challenge our current evaluation and reporting structures.

'Missions are about imaging what systems look like' says Professor of Innovation and Public Governance at University College London, Rainer Kattel, who works extensively on innovation policy and governance and whom we previously collaborated with on design for missions (Kattel, 2023). This statement makes it obvious that we cannot neatly steer after detailed project plans with a baseline, clear targets and clear deliverables, since we are aiming to change the underlying systems, we are operating in. We might, through our system analysis, for example, of purpose, power, relations and resources, have some promising and well-founded hypothesis of important goals to reach. But we are prone to be more open and flexible regarding how to move forward.

Søren Vester Haldrup, former Innovation Fund Manager at the United Nations Development Programme (UNDP), has been a pioneer in rethinking monitoring and evaluation (M&E) structures. As head of UNDP's M&E Sandbox, Haldrup has experimented with different evaluation and monitoring frameworks in collaboration with UNDP Country Offices and philanthropies such as the Bill & Melinda Gates Foundation.

We checked in with Haldrup to understand the essence of how measuring and evaluation practices are evolving today to accommodate for the nature of learning in systems change (Haldrup, 2024). Haldrup emphasizes that evaluation and monitoring has to change if we want to measure systems change. He depicts a development where retrospective reporting is toned down in favour of forward-looking and conversation-based learning. In more general terms, Haldrup describes a movement 'from a culture of compliance to a culture of learning' (Haldrup, 2023).

So how do we track progress if the goal is to create societal impact? Haldrup is consistently cautious to place effects (for example, reduced loneliness, increasing wellbeing, reduction of CO_2 emissions) as the target of progress reporting schemes. Effects such as these take a long time to materialize and are, thus, subject to much uncertainty and imprecision – these can be assessed post-facto and not as part of the intermediate progress reporting. Instead, learning in the interim should focus on capturing our initiatives' *contribution* to impact. Here, we find it helpful to revisit the *Impact Framework for Mission-Oriented Innovation* introduced as part of *Navigating Balance* that helps us break down a portfolio's strategic focus into learning questions and milestones.

We may also draw on experience from theoretical frameworks of systems theory, for example, from Leadbeater and Winhall's *Four Keys*, or some of the driving roles of systems change that we elaborate on in the coming navigation point, *Navigating*

Interdependence. With these as a backdrop, we can define our indicators and relate our learnings to whether the right conditions for change seem to evolve within the system as we intervene with it.

In organizing learning processes, Haldrup points us towards the Learning Framework Five Elements by Bertermann and Coffman (2024) as shown in Figure 7.3. This framework quite smartly puts together the different elements we have discussed throughout this chapter regarding learning and experimentation and adds an important extra layer: confirming and disconfirming evidence. As we plan our experiments, this helps us ensure we harvest the right data from the experiments to inform us if our assumptions are right or wrong. It can help us ask the right question in an interview or a survey, or look for a specific behaviour in a prototyping test – for example, as Comté Bureau looked for signs in the behaviour of young people, to see if they would actively use common spaces in a student housing setting.

As we sat down with Haldrup, we urged him to share some overall insights regarding learning that we, as pathfinders, can apply to slowly inspire and evolve a new monitoring and evaluation practice in this transition phase we are in today. A transition where the majority of the reporting systems are not necessarily ripe for this shift in culture and practice.

Haldrup argues that an important step that everyone can take today is to work on building a learning culture, by organizing learning loops, as we suggested with the Harvesting Learning model. Pathfinders should give priority to continuous learning sessions that facilitate a dialogue across the team on what they have learned (not achieved!) to identify whether this learning calls for new and different steps to be taken. Haldrup has tested different structures for these learning sessions with varying frequency depending on how 'deep' they want to dive into their learning. Lighter touch single loop learning, asking questions such as 'Are we doing things right?' can perhaps be a monthly event, whereas double and triple loop learning, 'Are we doing the right things?' and 'What is right?', should happen less frequently, perhaps every six months.

It is interesting for the pathfinder to gradually challenge incentives' structure, for instance, by revisiting and reformulating

Figure 7.3: The Learning Framework's Five Elements, an adaptation

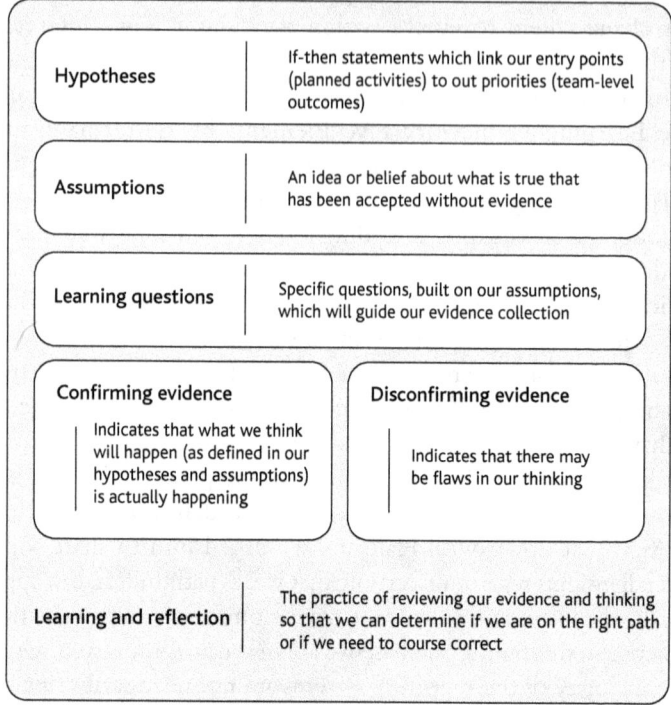

Note: The Learning Framework is a simple structure, composed of core 'building blocks' which will ensure that our evidence collection is focused and leans just as much on reflection and sense-making as gathering evidence.

Source: Bertermann and Coffman (2024)

indicators to assess if they encourage learning and are flexible enough to allow you and your team to adapt to what you have learned.

Creating systems change is fundamentally cross-sectoral and cross-disciplinary and only achieved through collective action. Therefore, Haldrup argues that it makes no sense to try to analyse one's individual attribution to specific effects or to take credit for making a specific change. Assessing the value of one's work should, therefore, focus on describing the contribution to change instead of one's attribution.

In some cases, it is possible to rethink your reporting format. This demands a solid understanding of who one is reporting to and an analysis of what kind of information they might need. Are there other ways one may convey that message of change? Haldrup challenges the inherent bias that numbers hold more value in evaluation than other forms of documentation. Other formats, such as stories, images or audio files, might better capture people's lived experience in a system in a way that numbers alone cannot. He proposes pathfinders should experiment with adding bits of these new elements to the report to see how it is received.

Lastly, Haldrup encourages us to think critically about the inherent power dynamics within monitoring and evaluation schemes, challenging today's practice. He argues that reporting today is driven by a top-down dynamic where authorities or foundations set the direction for change, and the organizations who actually drive the change processes continuously have to report upwards to authorities to document this particular change in order to ensure their livelihood as organizations: 'Who should define and describe the goal of the change we make?' asks Haldrup. 'What if it were the other way around where the people who are closest to the problems are given the resources and space to tackle them in the best way? Then the organisations who provide the funding should merely focus on providing the best framework conditions for this work' (Haldrup, 2024).

Let us stay with this refreshing sentiment and look to a concrete example in the Danish political landscape where a new initiative could potentially challenge the inherent power dynamics of political evaluation and decision processes; the work launched by the Danish think tank INVI that works to tackle *wild problems*.

Dynamic learning in political decision processes

The think tank INVI is determined to challenge some of the pitfalls of evaluation and decision making in Danish politics today. Roughly speaking, the Danish political landscape has grown accustomed to two distinct evaluation practices with very different paces (1) either super quick decision making through fast political responses to single issue topics, showing off political mandate and decisiveness, or (2) slowly by forming an expert committee for initiatives to thoroughly be examined, evaluated and reassessed. In the first case, we are effectively in danger of making bad decisions based on a fragile foundation and, in the last case, the process causes inertia and stagnation, impairing our ability to act. Neither seems satisfying. And neither process is sufficiently capable of bringing in learnings from the practitioners who are closest to the problems.

Therefore, INVI set out to create a model that could fundamentally shorten the distance between decision makers and practitioners, so that practitioners have an increased say and can provide ongoing feedback on how new legislation, politics or regulation work in their daily professional lives. This ensures that learning does not go to waste but is harvested and looped back into the system. In other words, the ambition behind INVI's model is to ensure a much richer data input, making us more knowledgeable about what happens when political reforms meet reality – and doing it faster and on a continuous basis.

INVI launched their new tool in the autumn of 2024. The setup is quite simple: it is a digital tool that systemically asks large groups of practitioners to give feedback on the practical implementation of new political reforms or legislation and to suggest improvements. For example, it could ask teachers to provide their professional input on how a school reform actually works in practice. The tool will then collect data at fixed intervals (for example, every three months), ideally from a very large group of practitioners across the country. It uses artificial intelligence to organize the rich data and generates patterns of learning. In this way, the tool bases its learning on collective intelligence from practitioners and professionals instead of engaging a few experts in a committee. You could think of it as a nationwide learning loop supported by artificial intelligence that continuously collects learning and organizes insights.

As Sigge Winther Nielsen, who leads the think tank, points out: 'We need to ask all those affected by, and actively working with the effects of policy every day, and we need to ask them continuously' (Esbjørnsen and Normann, 2024). Just like Haldrup proposes, this approach to learning, evaluation and decision making challenges the top-down logic that authorities should hold the answers to defining what works well and what does not.

The first results of INVI's tool have not yet come in, but the launch and the preceding thorough work reflect a growing interest in rethinking evaluation and making better use of the diverse knowledge that already exists. And it provides a concrete and data-driven learning mechanism for learning to be captured and utilized. In our view, it would be valuable to widen the scope of the model to involve the citizens. In this case, involving the students and their parents to include their perspectives and experiences, as, after all, they are the ones who experience and are impacted by the policies.

A different kind of leadership: towards a learning organism?

As we challenge measuring and evaluation and the incentives that drive learning in organizations today, it is not sufficient just to rethink our evaluation schemes. It is equally important to revisit how organizations operate and are ultimately being led. Traditional leadership practices and conventional organizational structures and incentives often challenge and even contradict the experimental, learning and abductive approach.

Fortunately, the way we see it, the role of the traditional leader is going through a shift these years – small cracks reveal a transformation in how we envision leadership. We experience leaders that move away from being the go-to person who knows it all, to being the facilitator who can open a space for questions and opportunities to flourish. This is a fortunate trend, because we need this change in mindset and leadership in order to succeed in transitioning our society and decentralizing the power and influence on the challenges we are trying to solve – together.

Unlocking a collective mindset

As we understand the nature of experiments, it becomes evident that leaders play a crucial role in driving progress and fostering a work environment that values these processes and the learning they bring. We find it essential for leaders to understand how to actively support employees or team members, especially when those employees face challenges or when the effectiveness of their processes is called into question, even by their own intrinsic doubt.

Design methods ask employees not to race to the finish line, not to converge on an answer as quickly as possible, and instead to widen the set of options – to go sideways for a while rather than forward. This can be difficult for people schooled in the need for efficiency, the importance of cost savings, the value of being lean, and so on. It can feel like 'spinning wheels' because it kind of is (Austin and Bason, 2019).

When leading the work of your pathfinding, it is vital to guide the team members and stakeholders in resisting the impulse to settle on solutions quickly. Care should be taken to support curious and impact-oriented individuals as they navigate the uncertainties and perceived ambiguities of the divergent process, leading by example through sharing one's own experiences of uncertainty while confidently endorsing the process.

We urge leaders to explore how to create an open and transparent environment where new insights are welcomed rather than feared. Failures are insights that drive new learning. It is vital that these new insights are framed as opportunities for progress and improvement, rather than as criticisms of past performance. Keep in mind that our hypotheses are based on assumptions, which means things we are not entirely sure about. Often, we discover something we did not think we would, which, on the surface, may seem like a mistake but which gives us a valuable opportunity to learn. By doing so, leaders can help their teams see these insights as chances to advance, leading to better outcomes for the organization as a whole.

This is no easy task, as Austin and Bason (2019) put it:

> Design approaches call on employees to often experience something that they have historically tried to avoid: failure. The aspects of these methods that involve iterative prototyping and testing work best when they produce lots of negative results, outcomes that show you what does not work. But piling up seemingly unsuccessful outcomes does not feel good to most people.

Leading collective change processes

To drive this behavioural change and support the learning culture of your work and organization, we encourage leaders to revisit the incentive structures of the organizations, such as KPIs, salaries and professional advancements, budgeting and feedback processes, asking which kind of behaviour they genuinely seek to reward.

Former owner and CEO of Skagerak, a furniture company, Jesper Panduro, had successfully transformed his company to become sustainable, more circular and B-Corp certified. We once asked him to point out the most influential event that drove a positive change in the organization. To him, it had been instrumental to establish a collective mindset in the company, mobilizing the entire staff to contribute to sustainable change. The single most important decision he made was to cancel individual bonuses. When we met for an interview, he said:

> We no longer have individual bonuses. We don't have any KPIs for how we perform. In my opinion, you only need KPIs if you have bad management skills. From now on, we will not measure people with numbers; we will measure people on how they perform as teams – we only have a collective bonus. Now, we are all in the same boat. It was difficult at first, but I see now that it changed the way we think and act. (Panduro, 2023)

Panduro stressed that this change drove people across the departments to work more closely together on implementing sustainability. Achieving cross-organizational collaboration is often a key challenge with sustainable transformation processes that tend to live isolated from core business. The change in leadership incentives concretely inspired new sustainability initiatives from salespeople and purchasers, for example, where and how to most efficiently and sustainably source materials in the organization. This collective initiative was new to the organization, as the employees had grown accustomed to steering after individual goals.

Iacopo Gronchi, PhD candidate at University College London, Institute for Innovation and Public Purpose and Demos Helsinki, who researches mission-oriented government models in policy, states that:

> There is a mismatch between the nature of our societal problems and the accountability systems we build to solve them. The former is permeated by strategic uncertainty, which demands managers to remain flexible and adapt their goals as they go along; yet the latter are characterised by static processes and demand clarity of outcomes even when this is not possible anymore. (Gronchi, 2023)

When we checked in with Gronchi, he also pointed to the significance of KPIs, asking:

> What happens when the intended goal cannot fully be synthesised into a narrow KPI? And what happens when bureaucrats try to achieve the KPI, but do not reflect on the broader implications of what they are doing – so that the KPI becomes a goal, rather than a device to pursue its underlying purpose? (Gronchi, 2023)

KPIs are one example of how organizational behaviour is steered, which underscores how fruitful it is for us to look with a critical eye, whether all the structures we put in place as leaders truly support collective learning and experimentation.

While the example of Skagerak might be one individual case, it highlights how strong a power organizational structures hold over organizational behaviour, and it underlines the necessity of shaking up the existing processes and incentive structures to encourage a new culture.

Behind the many organizational processes we have come across lies the embedded motivation for specific behaviour. We have met several organizations that are very explicit about being mission- or impact-oriented, innovative and collectively minded, both public and private. But as you analyse how their decisions are informed, the nature of their accountability systems, and how employees are rewarded, we find a gap between their articulated goals and the means applied to reach those goals.

There is a growing body of literature as well as an increasing number of good examples of leaders who have set out to design new organizations to accommodate experimentation and collective learning. Just like Panduro, they introduce tangible changes that serve as examples of how to reorientate hierarchy and accountability in the organization.

New organizational shapes take form

> Hierarchy is an outdated and ineffective way of organising human endeavours. (Laloux, 2014)

In our search for creating more impact and allowing for new logics, approaches and behaviour to gain ground, we, too, have experimented with organizing in new ways.

During a major reorganization and transition back in 2020, the Danish Design Center restructured itself to eliminate all hierarchies, requiring new pathways for decision making to be established, new roles to be distributed, and new ways of working to be integrated. The ambition was to significantly increase the societal impact of the programmes, missions and initiatives through new ambitious collaborations and partnerships.

For us as leaders, this demanded an almost complete reorientation of our roles and positioning and a whole new set of skills. Leadership became primarily about engaging, mobilizing and creating followership, both within the organization and externally, across the transition areas for which we were responsible.

It was no longer the decision-making authority given by our title as director that drove development but the ability to create followership. Undoubtedly, this organizational change demanded a lot of the organization, requiring energy, patience and empathy from the entire team – and for every one of us personally. Yet, it has been a powerful, valuable and rich learning experience. It revealed how new logics and discourses could foster far greater engagement, motivation and accountability in the organization. For instance, when the decision-making authority shifted to those with the subject- or project-specific knowledge, in this case, the project manager, decisions were made on a much more solid basis. As responsibility became more distributed, the organization moved much more flexibly, no longer held back by decision-making processes that did not add value or input to the work but only slowed and weakened the impact.

We saw how the organization transformed into a sensing organism, with far more receptors and inputs to base decisions and a much more distributed decision-making power to accelerate the impact. This allowed us to increase both our speed and our influence.

For a deep dive into the emerging new organizational and leadership practices, we recommend looking into the work of thinkers such as Frederic Laloux, Peter Senge, Sune Knudsen, Christian Bason and Brian J. Roberston, who, from different angles, stress the importance of distributed leadership and flat hierarchical structures and present concrete leadership models and cases that reward societal change processes.

What we have learned so far: navigating experiments

Navigating societal transitions requires accepting the unknown and the ambiguity that accompanies it. It calls for experiments we can learn from to unwind the unmanageable knot of challenges and move forward. Doing something small and lean helps us learn quickly for long-term systemic transitions.

We emphasized the need to be brave in addressing our problem and its opportunities in an experimental, playful and imaginative way, which challenges us as pathfinders and collaborators to remain open, curious, and responsive to the insights and developments that emerge during the process. Consequently, continuous learning and adaptation are essential to the pathfinder's everyday work.

We introduced a structure to learning *forward*: learning across portfolios. Portfolios are a way of organizing systemic interventions and learnings to gain progress and long-term impact. It means working simultaneously with multiple interventions and experiments with different partial goals. In that way, we can extract learning from individual interventions, initiatives, and even organizations and partnerships to feed into new experiments and interventions. It entails harvesting learning gradually at different scales: experiment, portfolio and system.

Part of finding new pathways is to challenge existing measurement methods. Therefore, we need to specify new and more collective impact goals. It entails that we, as pathfinders, and especially investors in both private, philanthropic and government sectors, must move away from traditional reporting and returns on investment. Instead, there is an important role in providing the necessary framework to drive change and create value. Moreover, we suggest shifting our perspective to focus on describing our contribution to change instead of claiming credit for change.

We have explored what it entails to adopt abductive reasoning and position learning as an energy flowing through our work. It is manifest that experimenting affects not just how we work but how we lead and design our organizations. The emerging new leader is someone who facilitates dialogues and exploration rather than providing the answers. The new leader embraces staying playful and serious. She creates psychological safety with lots of courage and vulnerability to experiment and learn what we do not know yet as a collective. This kind of transition leadership has the power to shape an organization where many more can enrich the basis for decision-making, and many more feel not only safe but obliged to contribute. It gives rise to the necessity of building organizations that function in new ways, where the incentives, structure and decision-making support learning, and organizations turn into learning organisms.

Navigating interdependence

> I believe in singing. I believe in singing together.
> Brian Eno, in Kahn, 2022

In the preceding navigation point, we have explored and challenged systems, structures, processes and ways of working. In this fourth and final navigation point, *Navigating Interdependence*, we arrive at the obvious, even banal, point that, in the end, every structure and every system consists of the same thing: people. Therefore, in our endeavour to create societal change, much of our success comes down to our ability to affect human behaviour and relationships.

As we mess with existing systems in our effort to create new ones, we challenge existing power dynamics and relationships, which often provoke resistance and may lead to conflict. As Leadbeater and Winhall put it: 'Conflict is an inevitable and important part of transition, and system innovators will not succeed if they are naive about the need to work with the resistance these efforts at change provoke' (Leadbeater and Winhall, 2020). The messy work of meddling with people – their personal whims, ideas, values, deeply rooted habits and personal idiosyncrasies – is often the hardest, most frustrating, and yet (if you ask us) the most enriching part of the job.

This navigation point, *Navigating Interdependence*, is about what happens when we move our focus from the analytic gaze of the logics and structure of systems towards the practical interaction and interference with cultures and human behaviour. In our conversations with systems innovator and urban planner Dan Hill, he highlighted the importance of the word *cultures*: 'I stress cultures to counterpoint the "systems" word, because systems can immediately sound very technical and problematically technocratic. Obviously, systems aren't that. In reality, systems can be highly qualitative and complex' (Hill, 2024a).

We subscribe to Hill's perspective, by stressing the argument that we are deeply dependent on the close interplay, collaboration and connectivity between people. In *Navigating Interdependence*, we will share ideas, dilemmas, reflections and theories that help us navigate the vital task of convening, connecting, mobilizing and inspiring people to collaborate for societal change.

Through the navigation point, we explore several different takes and dimensions on system actor collaboration by arguing and reflecting on the following:

- Why co-creation and collaboration is such an essential part of systems change.
- How we can map, analyse and understand the systems we are part of.
- How to facilitate participation and mobilization and to drive coalitions forward across different groups of people.
- Which essential roles people play in the cast-list for societal change.
- How to create organizational and governance structures around transition processes.

8

Weaving new patterns collectively

> I came up with this word *scenius* – the intelligence of a whole operation or group of people. I think that's a more useful way to think about culture. Let us forget the idea of 'genius' for a little while, let us think about the whole ecology of ideas that give rise to good new thoughts and good new work.
>
> Eno, 2009

Musician and producer Brian Eno's two quotes beautifully encapsulate the idea that creativity, originality or innovation seldom originate from the individual artist or genius but grow out of new connections and interactions among people in a community. In his book, *A Year of Swollen Appendices*, Eno refers to historical examples of the *scenius* from, for example, the New York City art scene in the 1970s or the Harlem Renaissance, where groups of artists, musicians, creatives and thinkers, through their interaction in physical common spaces, influenced and inspired each other to cultivate new cultural and artistic expressions.

This idea of *scenius* is alluring and an idea that fits well into how we should understand the potential of collaboration in systems. We can point to similar *scenius* movements outside the realm of the arts. A good example is the New Nordic Cuisine movement in Denmark that blossomed in the mid-2000s, where chefs and food experts met through creative experimentation and developed new values and practices around the meal. These new ideas of food were kicked off with the co-creation of the

New Nordic Cuisine Manifesto in 2004 by frontrunners from the gastronomy scene who met to innovate and experiment on the future of Nordic food. The manifesto committed actors in the Danish food industry to promote local, natural and seasonal produce as a foundation for cooking in restaurants and at home. The effects of this *scenius* were the profound transformation of the broad food culture in Denmark: a country previously known for its simple peasant dishes, today internationally renowned for its experimental *New Nordic* food culture.

Inspired by the notion of *scenius*, we want to highlight the power of collaboration and interaction among different people to spark new ideas and behaviour. When creating impactful system change, we stress that collaboration should happen widely across the system, transgressing the public, private and civic spheres and across different sectors and professional realms. This was the case with the New Nordic Cuisine movement. It not only stirred a new take on the good meal in Copenhagen's best restaurants but changed the terms of the food scene in Denmark. Thus, it inspired new practices in schools and homes, as well as impacting food, beer and wine production in Denmark and fundamentally influencing the values and norms around food (Thurfjell, 2020).

We state these two key arguments for why cross-sectoral system actor collaboration is a prerequisite for systems change: Collaboration sparks collective intelligence and innovation. As suggested by Eno, with *scenius*, several innovation experts argue for the importance of unlike minds coming together to ignite innovation by bringing different perspectives to existing problems or ideas. Leadbeater and Winhall also underpin the idea of collective innovation: 'Systemic opportunities require collaborative innovation because they require new connections to be made' (Leadbeater and Winhall, 2020: 12).

Collaboration facilitates the spreading, development and growing of new knowledge, practice, discourses and logics so that system opportunities can be adopted, further developed, scaled and mainstreamed. As Leadbeater and Winhall put it: 'System innovation is a cumulative, collaborative process which gathers its momentum from the degree of cooperation between many different players across all three levels of the system' (Leadbeater and Winhall, 2020: 43).

As we described in *Navigating Balance*, mission-oriented innovation is a political and economic framework that compels policy makers, companies and institutions to collaborate and co-create through bottom-up experimentation across society. In her book *Mission Economy: A Moonshot Guide to Changing Capitalism*, Mazzucato stresses that 'a stakeholder approach to value must begin with the recognition that value is collectively created by multiple groups, including businesses, workers and local and central governments' (Mazzucato, 2021: 168).

David Budzt Pedersen backs this sentiment up from a bottom-up perspective in the University of Aalborg's *Mission Guidebook*: 'By working actively with partners, crowdsourcing ideas, and co-creating solutions, the realm of influence can be expanded beyond business-as-usual. Partners can create leverage. Project consortia can create new pathways to impact' (Pedersen, 2024: 10).

We will return to the power of collaboration and participation and reflect on how this is best stimulated and anchored into lasting systemic change. But first, let us explore how to understand, visualize and assess the networks of people we are part of.

Learning from ecosystems

When thinking about networks of people and relationships, it is enlivening to gain inspiration from biology and the idea of *ecosystems*. The *ecosystem* is a biological term that describes how a community of living organisms such as plants, animals and microorganisms interact with each other and their physical environment as well as with non-living components – air, water and light from the sun. They create a dynamic cyclical system where energy and nutrients flow and resources are continuously recycled. This is a much-desired state yet starkly contrasting our dominant linear and extractive economy and production system.

Therefore, sustainability and systems thinkers continue to gain inspiration from biology and ecology due to the interconnected and regenerative nature of ecosystems. An example is Janine M. Benyus, who with her book *Biomimicry* (2002) insists that our innovation approaches learn from nature's processes. It is indeed fruitful to widen our scope from the narrow and somewhat transactional idea of stakeholders that we may have learned from, for example, Mendelow's well-known power-interest matrix from 1991, where stakeholders are assessed and analysed mainly in terms of their interests, influence and power.

Systems theory takes a broader and more holistic view of the actors in the system. Here, the system is understood as a complex network of interacting entities, including organizations, institutions, technologies, and individuals and their physical and environmental surroundings, collectively contributing to the development, diffusion and adoption of innovative solutions. The emphasis is not just on how stakeholders can be influenced but on how people and the system co-evolve and influence one another.

We find ourselves in a fascinating time where we witness a growing receptiveness towards this new and widened focus of our broader network and stakeholders. This is the case for companies and organizations proactively committed to the sustainable transition. We have, for example, interacted closely with companies engaged in the circular economy and have experienced how they are gradually opening their perspective to engage more broadly with the system around them.

Circular solutions – products or services – are dependent on and, thereby, enabled through, partnerships across a value chain that closely coordinates how materials travel from the initial design phase to its use-phase and finally – as late as possible – to its end-of-life phase. This affects how products are sourced, designed, distributed, used, collected, remanufactured, refurbished, reused, and so on. The interdependency in the value chain between numerous stakeholders – for example, the municipality to collect used products, distributors to track how goods circulate, or the user to repair a product – is evident. The movements towards new circular solutions force company leaders to initiate new partnerships across the value chain and out into the system, and it very distinctly reveals to us this huge interdependence among organizations in their endeavour to achieve impact together.

'We find ourselves moving away from transactional partnerships, based on the exchange of resources, to more integrated, value-based partnership, where the focus is on creating solutions together.' A participant expressed this at a workshop on circularity in the manufacturing industry held by the Danish Design Center. He was actively working with circularity in the wind power industry engaging in building partnerships with suppliers, distributors and researchers to achieve circularity in wind turbine components.

Along with this, the intensified focus on ESG - Environmental, Social and Governance reporting compels companies to account for their corporate activities both upstream and downstream in the value chain. To live up to these new requirements, companies are, for instance, increasingly expected to document all CO_2 emissions in three scopes: In Scope one: the direct emissions that the company controls; Scope two: indirect emissions associated with the purchase of electricity, steam, heat or cooling; and even Scope three: emissions that are not directly owned by the company but are indirectly emitted through the value chain. This information can only be obtained through practical dialogue and collaboration across often very complex and lengthy supply chains that cut across country borders and several organizations.

Additionally, through the social pillar, the S of ESG, companies must document how they enable ethics, justice and care for well-being, for instance, by measuring how the organization meets these social obligations in its work environment, through its operations and through transparent global supply chains. This new demand to comply with sustainability frameworks stresses that the growing tendency to engage in broad partnerships outside one's business or organization is not only relevant to inspire innovation. It is a necessity and an abrupt new reality for many companies today and will increasingly be so in the future when the regulatory and legislative requirements will intensify.

We deeply commend this new movement in the public and private sectors of increased value chain collaboration, new alliances and collaborations. Yet, there is no doubt that it increases the complexity for the people operating today's businesses and organizations. This complexity requires new skills aimed at collaboration, community-building, negotiation and communication across people with different interests, cultures and backgrounds.

So, let us move on to how to grasp and understand the broad networks we are a part of to address how to constructively intervene in them.

Mapping and analysing the system and its network

The exercise of mapping and analysing a system and its actors is a comprehensive venture that, in some ways, is never-ending. It is difficult to set clear boundaries around a system as one system quickly overlaps into another.

For instance, if we stay with the example of the circular transition in companies and try to map that system, it ties into several other systems outside the industrial domain. It could be the education system, where circular skills are trained, or the financial systems that are instrumental in incentivizing circular business models, or social systems that must encourage an alternative to the dominant throwaway culture among consumers. The idea that we can oversee, monitor and control systems is futile.

In our work, we have advised and participated in several design processes where we, together with teams, have tried to visualize the system we are part of and want to interact with. The outcome of this process, which is often a visual mapping of the system and its actors, has limited value in itself. In the efforts of fencing in the system, by mapping and analysing it, we are prone to reduce significant complexity. Yet, the process of understanding the system – the strategic dialogue and the visual act of illustrating roles and relationships – is invaluable and plays a crucial part in understanding the four keys of a system: its purpose, power, resources and relationships. Thus, the mapping deepens our understanding of the people, organizations and dynamics that characterize the system we work in and want to change.

There are different tools to map and visualize systems in co-creative processes that can guide you in this work. One can seek inspiration from Hill's and Vinnova's publication, *Designing Missions* (2022) as well as from the formative thinking of Bruno Latour and his ideas of Actor-Network Theory (ANT). We have also gained inspiration from some of the ideas behind the work of Mannervik and Ramirez. Their book, *Strategy for a Networked World*, introduces the idea of 'value-creating systems' as a way of of understanding the co-creation of value in networks (Mannervik and Ramirez, 2016). Whichever approach you apply, here are some reflections and points of attention that have been helpful in our own work.

Mapping out the system as is *before visualizing the system* to be

Our focus and analysis of a system varies significantly, depending on whether we address a current system or if we explore how to move the system forward. Therefore, we recommend splitting the analysis into two phases, where the first phase concentrates on the system *as is*.

Here, we raise our awareness of the power structures that shape the system today, the different roles and logics that define the system, the value created in the system, who creates it and, lastly, the operating governance models. We will want to ask ourselves: Who are the main characters, and what drives them – what are their incentives and motives? Who holds the power, and who has the resources? Which are the dominant relationships, and what value exchange are they based on?

Our questions are different when we move on to the system *to be*. Here, our focus is on how to move the system forward. This could be questions such as: What actors could play a different, more value-creating role? Are there actors who need to play a different role and actors who are outside the system but need to be drawn in? What could be new drivers of value in relationships? How can new and other kinds of resources be unlocked?

Looking for different kinds of power – both hard and soft

As we analyse the different roles of actors in a system, one might look for the people or institutions that hold power in the current system and be concerned about how to access and influence that power. Here, we suggest a multifaceted view of power, acknowledging that power comes in many shapes.

The obvious power might be the formal, *hard*, hierarchical power that is held by people in government, finance or large corporations. However, it is equally interesting to understand how *soft* power is dominant in maintaining and evolving our systems. As Leadbeater and Winhall put it, soft power sets 'our culture and values, the language and concepts we have available to see the world and imagine alternatives. ... Soft power is the ability to get others to buy into the values which keep you in power' (Leadbeater and Winhall, 202: 17).

To affect these values and norms, we may reframe these in new narratives, as explored in *Navigating a New Story*. Power is not a static concept held by the few. Power can change based on group dynamics, cultural movements and abrupt societal changes. And it is interesting to keep an eye out for these different power dynamics. Just think of how one teenager, through her Fridays for Futures school strikes, influenced the global climate change conversation.

You are not the centre of the world; you are a player in a network

'None of us see the system. We see our own part based on our own background and history. And we all think we see the most crucial part' says system scientist Peter Senge (2006). Systems are complex, interconnected and decentralized. The idea that there is a centre everything revolves around, or that one perspective sheds a clearer light on a system than others, simply does not fly.

Therefore, as we map out systems, we should refrain from the urge to place ourselves or our organization in the middle of the system and then draw out links to stakeholders from here. We want to look at the system as open-minded as possible, understanding what is at stake while toning down our biases and vested interests. When we have gained a deeper understanding of the specific system, we can move on to exploring what our personal, organizational or collective (if we represent a partnership, group or alliance) role is in contributing to the system's dynamics in a favourable and meaningful way.

The analysis will never be conclusive

Identifying relevant stakeholders can be a comprehensive and, potentially, never-ending activity, where you may continuously discover new stakeholders or relationships that might inform the system somehow, thus expanding your stakeholder mapping to an endless spiderweb. Yet, the purpose here is not to get too conclusive. We cannot draw the perfect picture of the system, so let us not try. However, we can aim for a solid starting point for analysing and understanding the specific dynamics of the system we navigate.

Instead of painting the finished picture, one can use a system analysis as an ongoing tool to revisit when addressing strategic reflections. It may be helpful to break down stakeholders into clusters or groups depending on their role in the system and their different ways of contributing to change. We will unfold these roles in the coming pages.

With the system map and the analysis of the actors and how they interact, pathfinders will have a much better starting point for how to intervene in the system and how to facilitate new partnerships or alliances that may move the system forward.

Driving collaboration through design

In previous work, Julie once attended an interdisciplinary workshop with fellow experts and practitioners in the circular economy and sustainability field. Here, the group had to introduce themselves with name, position and which education they would choose to take if they were to build on top of their existing profession. It was striking to hear several engineers and political scientists turn to psychology. They all expressed their eagerness to understand more deeply the emotional and cognitive triggers that drive people to act as they do. Then, at some point in the conversation, an esteemed mechanical engineer recognized for achieving impressive results in large corporations within digital and sustainable transition made the humble contribution: he would like to educate himself in collaboration. He did not know where to train for it or if such an education existed, but he felt it was a necessary premise for achieving sustainable change. When Julie had the opportunity to speak, she told him to start studying design.

While there are many branches and practices within design, some more participatory than others, it is widely recognized today that the design disciplines offer concrete ways of facilitating collaboration among people. Design and domains such as anthropology, psychology, sociology and pedagogy can help us provide the necessary participatory scaffolding for systems change.

Ezio Manzini, honorary professor in design, puts collaboration and empathy at the heart of the design practice in an interview on design for social innovation:

> For me ... the more important thing, is that those who wish to operate in the design field for social innovation must adopt a positive approach toward people and society. They also need to research and recognise the social resources that are already active or could be activated in a given place and time. (Muratovski, 2023: 78)

In our view, design's power as a convener and collaborator is due primarily to the following three points.

Design gives priority to human needs and conditions

Terms that describe design, such as *user-driven*, *human-centric* and *empathetic*, reveal design's determination to uncover and respond to human needs in the development of solutions. Designers have a wide range of methods to go beyond people's obvious and articulated wants. For example, by immersing themselves in their environment, by bringing in their voices through participatory processes, or by continuously testing assumptions, ideas and solutions with people to collect feedback.

Design processes are based on collaboration and participation

Yet, design is not merely focused on understanding the needs and values of people but has emerged as a collaborative practice insisting that solutions to complex issues should be created together with the people for whom the solutions are targeted. Therefore, the focus is on the involvement of users, partners, suppliers and other stakeholders through the entire design process – through both the divergent and convergent processes (Bason, 2016). *Co-creation* is the umbrella term for these collaborative strategies, where the designer involves multiple stakeholders (end-users included) working together to produce a shared outcome.

Tangible prototypes and visual imagery aids collaboration across different people

By insisting on the visual and tangible, design supports people from different backgrounds in establishing a common ground and a shared language. As we learned from the examples from the Danish government authority process, Boxing Future Health and Vorby, these processes created a shared point of reference and served as boundary objects for a shared language and narrative. Designers do this by visualizing processes, continuously sketching ideas and solutions, designing visual tools that support discussions or bringing in imagery and tangible objects as prompts to spark imagination.

The conductor, the steward and the shepherd

> The designer's job is to be a bit like the conductor in an orchestra. I do not mean that in a hubristic way because in an orchestra, the most important people are the first violin or the singers in the opera – they are the superstars. The conductor literally does not make a sound, personally! The job is just to make sure that everything is hanging together and that things are connected. That it adds up to something. (Hill, 2024a)

Talking to Hill, he used the imagery of the conductor to illustrate the distinct role of strategic design in collaborative processes around systems change. This image corresponds to several similar ideas we have seen design experts apply: the *steward* who, through a facilitative role, is a steward of innovation or shepherd of the transition (Brown, 2009) or as someone who *orchestrates* or *facilitates* change. The essential point is that leading co-creation is not about walking in the front or steering the wheel. It is about creating room for people and organizations to *actually* take ownership of a problem and its many opportunities.

Being the *conductor* or *steward* is a very proactive role. As Winhall insisted through our conversation with her, it is not a neutral position, where the job merely is to make sure that all voices are heard, and all input is collected:

I have met designers who see their role as a neutral facilitator. I don't really believe it's possible to be neutral in this work. You must take responsibility in some way for shaping direction. You are not just a group process facilitator; you're also trying to connect the micro to the macro, spot where the energy is and draw out what is actionable. Driving this kind of collaboration is, in a way, a process of collective discernment: you are tuning in to what could be system-shifting. Through dialogue and participation, you build up a picture together of what is noise and what is signal. And you pick out the signal and try to build momentum around it. (Winhall, 2024)

The pathfinder's role here as an orchestrator of collaboration processes can pick up participatory and creative elements from the designer's toolbox to spur contribution and engagement from the participants. Yet, it is of equal importance to keep a systems mindset in the back of one's mind to understand where the potentials are, for example, building a new purpose, creating new relationships in the system and to enhance or weaken different dynamics depending on their perceived potential. Indeed, to the extent that these dynamics can be controlled.

Releasing control

Engaging people in a creative process where you give them a voice and agency inevitably require you to let go of control.

An example of this loss of control was introduced to us in our conversations with Transformation Lead, Mikkel Holst, who co-leads the transformation of the infamous Pusher Street in Copenhagen's 'Freetown' Christiania. Christiania is an intentional community located in the borough of Christianshavn in Copenhagen. It was established in a squatted military base as a free and open town in the 1970s and has since operated with its own flag, rules and a consensus-based communal governance structure. It is a culturally diverse place, full of artistic expression and a popular tourist destination. But with the open cannabis trade on the main street, Pusher Street, Christiania has also become infamous for the growing crime and conflict among the drug dealers in the city, which has cast deep shadows on the Freetown Christiania and on the City of Copenhagen.

A breakthrough happened in the spring of 2024, when Christiania, in close collaboration with the police and the City of Copenhagen, finally shut down the organized drug market in Pusher Street for good. The street was even dug up due to the renovation of water pipes. This was a planned conjunction of events since the street became completely inaccessible. Mikkel Holst and a local Christianite (a Christiania resident), Risenga Manghezi, has since been hired by Christiania to lead the transformation of Pusher Street to become and open, creative and inclusive crime-free space.

Holst describes Christiania as a place where the social fabric is worn from many years of conflict regarding organized crime in Pusher Street. This has led to a democracy that struggles to make fast and necessary decisions and requires extreme amounts of relational work from individuals to achieve results. At the same time, there is an expectation and constant push from the state and city government for an accelerated transformation, which demands of Holst and Manghezi to achieve visible and comprehensive results quickly.

> When the project started, we had little more than a tight deadline and a more or less imaginary project plan with little to no concrete mandate from the community. Combined with an – at times – aggressive opposition from people who had lost their livelihood because of the closure of the drug market, one of the first things we agreed on was to focus our resources where the positive energy was, no matter how small. We supported almost any activity that could signify a change – concerts, exhibitions, art projects. This bought us time to learn from these activities, but also to identify key actors, build trust and simply gather energy for bigger and more difficult decisions. (Holst, 2024)

Holst and Manghezi rapidly had to be able to change their plans if new projects and unexpected ideas emerged from other actors, such as when a group wanted to turn their office building into a laundry and community hub. Today, their office is in temporary containers.

The consensus-based decision structure has also meant that they had to rethink some of the conventional tools in urban planning to guide the decision process. Holst explains:

> At Christiania, we do not have the decision hierarchy we are accustomed to in urban planning. Therefore, impulsive ideas for an indoor or outdoor space can instantly shortcut a strategic discussion. One of the things we do to inform decisions is to work virally with the ongoing internal conversation at Christiania. We test ideas and present dilemmas to the many Christianites we meet every day, and we in turn, convey and amplify ideas and dilemmas they present to us. Suddenly the ideas might live their own life, and new ideas mature. (Holst, 2024)

Holst's story is fascinating, because so many aspects are drawn to the extreme: an engaged, but very diverse group of Christanites operating with a completely flat hierarchy, colliding with threats from organized crime, a strong political push from the state and the local city government to deliver results, a distinct cultural and historical heritage and the experimental and colourful ways of artistic expression that characterize Christiania.

While the case may be exceptional, it also tells us something more fundamental about human behaviour: That we cannot successfully steer and coerce people into doing something they do not want. And we need to create the right conditions and the capacity for engagement to grow. We can inspire and motivate, but if we are to genuinely create lasting change after our efforts subside, we must follow the energy, read people's motivation, build capacity and plan after the initiatives of the people we engage with.

9

Building coalitions

The transition to a circular economy starts with a coalition of the willing and a shared sense of urgency. No actor can realise a circular initiative alone.
> Jacqueline Cramer, in Wadhwani, 2022

Professor, author and former Dutch Minister of Housing, Spatial Planning and Environment Jacqueline Cramer has been a frontrunner in advancing the circular transition in the Netherlands through an approach she refers to as *network governance*. With network governance, she refers to a way of building *coalitions of the willing*, where each partner fulfils a specific function and where the alignment through *transition brokers*, enable both worlds, public and private, to strengthen the positive forces in society (Cramer, 2020).

While her experience and examples relate to the circular economy, they are just as applicable to other systemic challenges in the broad sphere of societal change. In her book *How Network Governance Powers the Circular Economy*, Cramer shares ten guiding principles for bottom-up circular initiatives that should figure as additions to conventional public governance processes. Cramer describes a focused, iterative process that she has now applied in several areas, for example, the concrete and clothing industry in the Netherlands.

When Cramer describes the *coalition of the willing*, she points to the importance of including willing and able individuals in systemic change processes representing the sector where changes need to be made. In assembling this group, she is careful about selecting the right people who are both willing and able to work with sustainable transformation, zeroing in on people who are open to opportunities rather than listing obstacles.

'I hate to talk about barriers', Cramer candidly told us as we interviewed her:

> Everybody is a champion in mentioning barriers. And the barriers they mention are always things that they do not want to take responsibility for. Systems are rigid, and many people depend on each other to keep the system as it is. They try to make the changes compatible with the system. Then what you get is incremental change. (Cramer, 2024)

By targeting the right and willing individuals and building a strong sense of common urgency, Cramer can facilitate a dedicated and collaborative process and create progress within the group. For instance, in her work chairing a circular economy working group for the Netherlands' national Concrete Agreement, she managed to reach agreement around ambitious targets for the circular transition of the concrete industry together with the sector. One example is developing 100 per cent circular concrete and making material passports for buildings and construction obligatory by 2030.

It is evident that while Cramer's approaches are bottom-up and her coalitions are clearly focused, small and targeted, her long-term ambitions are to mainstream circularity broadly in the market and the sector. But she does this in a specific order: she starts by building proof of concept through these targeted coalitions with the willing actors in the system. When they have reached agreements and committed to the transition through concrete ambitions, they can move forward with implementing, adapting and scaling circularity in the industry.

For achieving these results, Cramer highlights the importance of interacting with the national government:

> When a transformational change is needed, as in the case of the circular economy, the government cannot just leave implementation to the market. Firstly, this

> is because the mainstream market has too many stakes in its current, mostly linear economy. Secondly, the market cannot make the system change alone (...) The government must keep in close contact with the network partners and maintain equal footing with them. (Cramer, 2020: 167)

The Cramer quote above is emphasizing that this networked way of working represents a dramatically different role for many national government actors.

In the mission-oriented work we have been part of, we made a distinction similar to Cramer's between stakeholder groups. We separated our stakeholder groups into two categories: (1) the *innovators* and (2) the *sustainers*. During our system map analysis, we asked ourselves: Who has interests in innovating the systems? And who is most concerned about sustaining it because they rely on it and are, therefore, reluctant to change?

Both stakeholder groups are equally significant, but it is essential to treat them differently and invite them into different stages of the process and for different tasks. The *innovators* are similar to Cramer's coalitions of the willing: people or organizations who experience the same urgency to change the system as we do. This urgency can arise from many different angles: from new political priorities, pressure from the market, innovation opportunities or from a personal dedication to deal with the gravity of the societal challenge.

Aligning on the urgency to create change is pivotal. 'It is essential that despite any differences in motives, participants have enough in common to take collective action' says Cramer (2020: 123). She also underlines that the smaller the group and the more targeted the issue, the easier it is to find the common ground for a joint ambition. Just imagine if Cramer had assembled the whole concrete sector of both *sustainers* and *innovators* in the Netherlands. We imagine the process would be very slow and terribly unproductive.

Cramer shared an insight with us when co-creating a joint ambition in these coalitions: A high and bold ambition serves as a much stronger driver instead of setting more short-term goals:

> When we talk about *goals*, people automatically lower the bar and think in terms of the incremental changes

that they are able to make within their organisation. I said, stop talking about goals, instead, let's talk about the ambition we want to reach, whether we reach it in 2030 or 2033. And that worked much better. Then they began to think about innovation. (Cramer, 2024)

Cramer's point here resonates well with the points we make about navigating a new story and setting direction for missions. By creating an aspiring new narrative for change in the system, we open the space for several new opportunities and possible solutions to flourish.

The other group of people, the *sustainers*, are people or organizations where either their personal inclination is too resistant towards innovation, or their organizational interests are too much in opposition to the goal. These stakeholders should not be ignored. Often, they have a massive influence on the system and are gatekeepers to mainstreaming change. This could be trade organizations or representatives of policy administrations. It could also be private companies relying economically on the existing system, where their very existence is at risk.

As Cramer suggests, these actors should be engaged not in the innovative space of the coalition, but when commitment or proof of concept has been achieved by the *innovators*. The commitment from a coalition of *innovators* can be powerful in creating a renewed sense of pressure among the *sustainers* to oblige with new demands for changes.

This was the case with the Concrete Agreement when Cramer chaired the circular economy group, which led to the commitment to ambitious targets for circular concrete (Cramer, 2020: 68). For each target, the coalition described a series of actions: governmental barriers that should be removed, a monitoring scheme, and a renewed governance structure that should be put in place to meet the conditions of the new target, for example, creating 100 per cent circular concrete in 2030. With these actions, Cramer could then move on with the execution of the Concrete Agreement through subsequent stages of building and scaling up, engaging stakeholders broadly from the concrete sectors (the *sustainers*).

Fortunately, the two distinct roles – the *innovators* and the *sustainers* – are not fixed groups. With the constantly evolving change in politics, the economy and social developments, political agendas and interests regularly change. What one day seems wild and overly ambitious can quickly become a new norm. Take, for example, the Danish national goal to reduce CO_2 emissions by 70 per cent in 2030 compared to the 1990 levels. In 2019, a 60 per cent reduction proposal had been put forward from a group of left-wing political parties with support from environmental groups. However, this proposal was deemed too ambitious and unrealistic by conservative political parties and the industry and voted down. Not more than a year after, a 70 per cent (!) goal was implemented in Danish law with the Danish Climate Act in 2020. Today it is broadly politically backed by parties from both the left and right.

The power of intermediaries

Cramer is a captivating person to follow. Her role in the Dutch ecosystem is quite remarkable as she skilfully bridges the gap between the different sectors and domains she engages in through her transition work. And Cramer is indeed a unique character. She is a professor, a former minister, and has worked with sustainability in the industry and non-governmental organizations. There is no doubt that her personal experience, education and network help Cramer speak the language, understand the hidden interests and read the cultural codes of the different environments she engages with.

Cramer herself argues that a critical challenge in her work is often the group's lack of ability to understand each other from across policy, academia and industry. When taking on this challenge, she calls her role that of the *transition broker*. She argues that this role is crucial to drive systemic innovation processes forward and to act as a translator and orchestrator of systemic change.

> Transition brokers can help align all relevant stakeholders. Sometimes a transition broker is just one person; at other times it is an organization. It is the broker's role to orchestrate the transition process, which is something they can accelerate from a neutral position. They are trustworthy and try to build coalitions with parties

that are willing to take transformative steps forward. ... Their tasks are to develop proper interfaces between the different actors, help satisfy the necessary preconditions and make sure that impactful circular initiatives can be established. (Cramer, 2020)

The role of the *transition broker* can be played by many different people. Cramer stands out because she personifies the bridging of domains and perspectives as she can see the challenge from both a policy, business, research and civic perspective. But the brokering can be conducted by a broad palette of individuals or groups who contribute with different angles and have this ability to translate, the pathfinder included. We have already introduced you to a few transition brokers, whom we see as pathfinders: Rowan Conway who chaired the Sustainability PLF's task force, Mikkel Holst in Christiana, and ourselves, through the role we took in projects like Boxing Future Health, Vorby and Decoupling 2030.

We see a pattern here. The ability to transform systems rarely emanates from established organizations, because they are so deeply embedded in the logics of the inherent system. Therefore, different brokers emerge from the system: individuals, specific organizations or alliances that take a more impartial position in the ecosystem and can convene actors around a shared ambition. A consistent character trait to many of these is that they are outsiders to the system but have sufficient understanding and knowledge of the problem and its opportunities to legitimize their orchestrating role.

The cast list for societal change

Besides the transition broker, there are several important roles to play in the band of systems change. We already introduced four roles described by the British Design Council: the *system thinker*, the *leader and storyteller*, the *designer and maker*, and the *connector and convener* that we related with the role of pathfinding for systems change. We also draw on the work of Winhall and Leadbeater, who introduce 12 roles for systems change.

Winhall and Leadbeater introduce a vital character in the cast of systems innovation who is a well-known figure from the innovation sphere, *the entrepreneur*, who dares to build new and visionary concepts on the fringes of our existing systems. 'They are the pioneers marking out the territory of the new system' (Leadbeater and Winhall, 2020: 40). Their achievements can both be within technology or solutions as we know them from the startup world, but they also operate in the field of social or environmental innovations. A technological example is Wikipedia that, after its birth in 2001, gradually transformed the landscape of information access, making it more inclusive, dynamic and collaborative across society.

Winhall and Leadbeater also highlight another role that should be noticed: *the inside-outsider*. The inside-outsiders 'recognise the challenge to the existing system they are part of and so open it up to new ideas, from outsiders, to help a new, different system emerge from within the shell of the old. These people who span the boundaries of the current system play a critical role' (Leadbeater and Winhall, 2020: 40). Inside-outsiders can help identify openings for new solutions and ways of working, paving the way for new transition paths. You can say they help perforate the system, enabling outsiders to present new opportunities into the system. When it comes to systems change, it is key not to downplay the importance of these people who act within the system, understand the existing system flaws and are able to look for loopholes. While several outsiders may have the *right* ideas for change, they are dependent on the adaption of these ideas in the system – for the ideas to move from being right to becoming *possible*.

Holst, in Christiania, underlines his deep dependency on his partner, the Christiania resident Manghezi – as an invaluable inside-outsider, who navigates the culture of Christiania as he tries to make room for small pockets of change:

> The discussions at the decision meetings in Christiania are hard to access for outsiders like me. Understanding the intricacies of their democracy is crucial to know where to give support, where to give push-back and when to grasp the possibility for a decision. The project would simply not be possible without this combination of an inside and an outside perspective. (Holst, 2024)

Figure 9.1: Outsiders and insiders

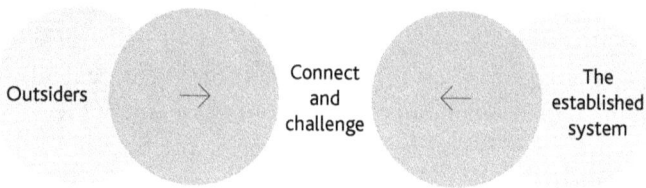

It is through the constant interaction at the fringes of the established system that the insiders and outsiders interact and engage to explore, challenge and shape new pathways. One can view it as a dynamic pull towards one another and to a new, not yet defined, space that eventually becomes a new system or a space that will gradually be absorbed by the established system. This dynamic is illustrated in Figure 9.1.

As we highlight some of the main characters for societal change, the cast list for societal transition is wide and diverse, and there are several roles people can play leveraging their unique positions and skills. Entrepreneurs need backup and support from funders and their ideas need to be commissioned by organizations with resources. Knowledge from academia, science, history and culture must be brought forward to give perspectives on the decisions we take. Arts play a role in provoking, challenging norms and inspiring critical thinking, translating abstract visions and ideas into something tangible. New frameworks should be presented that assess, legitimize and monitor the progress we make of our new initiatives. And so on.

The cast is limitless, and, in our view, everyone can and should play a part in bettering the system. Everyone should care for and be aware of their contribution. The grand challenges are shared, and we must solve them together through collective action. As societal change happens over long periods of time, the many characters might not meet and interact at the same time, and their current relationships might not be immediately apparent. But as Winhall and Leadbeater argue, it is helpful to make these roles recognizable to help us make the necessary connections between our individual position and our connections with and contributions to societal change (Leadbeater and Winhall).

A fitting backdrop to weave together the threads of our roles is to introduce a last, somewhat antagonistic character: *the retreater*. Retreaters are people who acknowledge that through their behaviour or position, they contribute to maintaining a system that is outdated and in opposition to the development of new opportunities and ideas. So much emphasis today is put on the innovators who drive change, yet so much opportunity is locked in by people in power who constrain new movements from flourishing. Stepping back and down, for example, in decision or development processes, is a courageous act that needs to be applauded and supported. We do not mean to imply that specific kinds of people are unwelcome in the cast list for societal change makers, but it is cardinal for every individual who holds power to be alert as to whether they have the skills, ability or motivation to let new processes and ideas replace older ones. If not, their important task is to pave the way for others.

As the increasingly complex poly-crises unfold, which have profound consequences for younger and future generations, we experience an acute awareness of the concept of power and influence on decision making, especially in younger generations. They do not wish merely to be included; they seek influence and power. Influence over the decisions that will impact their generation and the generations to come. One of today's climate activists, Elise Sydendal, says, 'Power is a zero-sum game. If we, the youth, are to have a seat at the table, someone needs to give up theirs' (Sydendal, 2024).

An example of a *retreating* character is CEO Uffe Lyngaae of the communication agency Publico, who decided to step down as personal manager in his business with the statement 'I have fired myself as boss'. He states:

> I have simply misjudged myself as a manager and realised too late that modern leadership (especially of younger colleagues) is more than just openness to potential inquiries (I kid you not, that has been my approach!). Modern leadership of talented knowledge workers apparently involves, among many other things, being able to provide professional support, feedback, backing, recognition, and clarity. And I have been far

from the best at this, even though I was the one who founded the company. As if that should qualify me for leadership. (Lyngaae, 2024)

This critical assessment of Lyngaae's capabilities, motivation, interests and biases as he lets go of some of his power, is something to be recognized.

The need for multiple capabilities

Societal transition calls for multiple capabilities within the system, an increased awareness of the various competencies and resources needed, as well as the knowledge of or sensitivity to when they are required. There are, of course, several capabilities that need to be present in a systemic transition, yet we prefer to highlight the capabilities that, in our view, are overlooked: the role and the capacity of philanthropists, citizens and businesses.

First, let us look to the power of philanthropy, apart from the obvious and essential role of providing risk capital for the transition.

Philanthropy – patient money

Here, we bring forward an example from the Danish political scene with the approval of the Danish Green Tripartite in the summer of 2024. The Danish Tripartite is a reform that introduces a new tax on livestock emissions but also commits to a massive restructuring of the Danish landscape. Some 140,000 hectares of existing farmland is to be converted into carbon-rich lowland soils and 250,000 hectares of new forest will be established. In the small country of Denmark this means that more than 15 per cent of the total Danish agricultural land is to be transformed into forest and nature. Along with this, the reform includes new regulation of land areas to achieve less polluted and more ecological and biodiversity rich waterlands.

This historic reform was reached with parties representing the state, the agricultural industry and nature. The reform was initially kicked off as a tripartite process to agree on a politically very sensitive topic: putting a tax on livestock emissions – focusing primarily on climate reductions. Yet, it ended up as a broad, holistic and cross-sectoral agreement with an approach to land management that is built on consideration for both nature, biodiversity, drinking water and an efficient and modern food production system (State of Green, 2024). Ultimately, if successfully implemented, it will dramatically redraw the Danish agricultural system as we know it today.

It is interesting to follow the work of the Danish Philanthrophic Organisation, Realdania, that has played a unique role leading up to the Green Danish Tripartite. Back in 2014, Realdania was a central and crucial capacity in the very early stages of rethinking how we allocate and utilize land in Denmark by initiating the long-term 'collective impact' collaboration around *The Future of Sustainable Landscapes* (Realdania, 2022).

In our conversation with the head of Realdania's collective impact initiatives, Mette Margrethe Elf, who has been partly responsible for Realdania's ongoing investments and work on land use in Denmark, she highlights how Realdania spearheaded a new type of modern commission work – rethinking how to gather stakeholders to collaboratively develop joint answers to challenging societal issues (Realdania, 2023). The topic of future land use is critical in the small country of Denmark where more than 60 per cent of all land is applied for agricultural use. This makes Denmark one of the most cultivated countries in the European Union, putting massive pressure on every bit of land.

Realdania gathered a broad alliance of organizations representing different interests and perspectives on how to approach the sustainable use of land in the country, with representatives from government, agriculture and nature. Solutions were to be developed in the collaboration between landowners, local communities and landscapes.

> Traditional commission work often ends with a report and, at best, recommendations, which political leaders bring into decision-making rooms. What we did in our work when we initiated it in 2014 was to launch a series of tests and pilots to demonstrate what it could look like if we renegotiated the purpose of land in Denmark, says Elf. (Elf, 2024)

Over an eight-year process, the initiative explored different solutions through pilots that tested how to apply acreage in new ways and as a driver in the green transition. This led to the development of a new tool: multipurpose land allocation, exploring how a new use of land can help obtain climate, nature and environmental targets while creating benefits for local communities, farmers and the agricultural industry (Realdania, 2023).

Elf emphasizes that it is the parties and organizations behind the Danish Green Tripartite who can take the credit for the creation of the new political reform. In our view, there is, however, no doubt about the crucial role Realdania has played in planting the seeds for the result today. The philanthropic organization has played a vital part in providing patient funding and allocating the necessary time, resources and research to properly understand and work with the challenge. As a non-political stakeholder they could hold a third space across a diverse partner group with conflicting interests. And by persistently supporting the initiative through experiments and pilots they were able to identify concrete steps forward into a new take on land-use.

Seen from a systems perspective, Realdania's collective impact work led to a repurposing of the use of land which has led to the current reform that changes the role of the farmer, whose main purpose was to grow crops and produce food, into a *land manager* whose purpose now can both be the production of food, nature and biodiversity.

'We need to increasingly place the Danish farmer at the centre as a land manager – regardless of whether the area is forest, nature, or fields – and shift from a narrative in the debate that it is agriculture versus nature to one where agriculture is together with nature', says Søren Søndergaard, Chair of the Danish Agriculture and Food council in a *Zetland* article (Hebsgaard, 2024).

It cannot be ignored that the Danish Green Tripartite draws on many of the components that were designed during Realdania's facilitation. This example underscores the point that change is not solely driven by political decision-makers but happens alongside and around us through the constant maturing of change in society.

Citizens and business – an unleashed capability

For our point on the power of the citizens and businesses, let us look to Jon Alexander, who advocates for shifting the societal narrative from seeing people as consumers to recognizing them as active citizens. In his opinion, the capabilities we need for transition are already there – we just need to unleash them through a shift in how we view the world. His work focuses on empowering individuals to participate more fully in democratic processes, encouraging businesses, governments and organizations to embrace a *citizen* mindset rather than treating people as passive consumers who must conform to industry and policy rules. According to Alexander, change needs to happen not just within existing policy frameworks but through fostering genuine participation at all levels, from local initiatives to business practices. He insists that 'communities *are* powerful, they do not need to be empowered, they just need *not* to be disempowered. What we need is to acknowledge, celebrate and support the power that is immanent in them' (Alexander, 2024).

Alexander points to something interesting here: businesses are not just economic entities but integral players in societal transitions. When adopting a citizen mindset and prioritizing societal and environmental goals, businesses can foster more participatory and democratic societies. He suggests that businesses need to rethink their relationship with people as consumers to active citizens who can contribute to societal well-being. This shift can lead to more innovative and sustainable business models.

And here lies an overlooked potential. Even though we can agree on businesses' role in shaping our society with jobs, community, direction and, in many Western countries, as a prerequisite for a functioning welfare state, the time may have come to expand their role or at least the notion of their impact.

When interviewing Christian Bason on his perspectives on important roles and capabilities of a system in transition, he interrupts himself in the middle of explaining the expanded role of the philanthropic foundations. He then adds that in his many years of experience in leading organizations that work for societal change and public sector innovation, businesses have always been underestimated resources. He points to businesses' often overlooked capacity and impactful role: 'We should be acutely aware how much private companies affect our society and everyday life' (Bason, 2024).

We find ourselves aligned with Bason's train of thought. Businesses' role and contributions are underappreciated elements in the significant transformative processes of societal transition, and so is their responsibility. The capabilities they bring into the system are multifaceted. The obvious points referenced for years are that they bring valuable innovation, knowledge and speed to the work of societal change. But, for us, it goes beyond that: Large and small businesses can lead and engage in advocacy for societal change agendas and drive or participate in partnerships and alliances. They have the potential, and, thus, also the obligation, to set new agendas across the supply chain and introduce new requirements for subcontractors. Hence, businesses can introduce new solutions that present new system opportunities (infrastructure, technology, services, products) and, thereby, mainstream new approaches and discourses by pushing products and services into the market.

Fortunately, we do see signs of businesses embracing these emerging new roles and contributions as ripples on the surface. One interesting example among many is the Norwegian startup Nyby, which 'helps accelerate the transition to sustainable welfare' by assisting hospitals, municipalities and organizations in tailoring local collaborative networks for task-sharing, to increase overall care capacity and to increase welfare, happiness and quality of life (Nyby, 2024). Nyby provides a service through an app that helps municipalities organize welfare services through direct connections between contributors and those in need of assistance. Employees in the municipalities, with their work phones, announce the relevant need, which is sent as a message directly to those who can contribute, for example, volunteer centre, unemployment office, coordinator of internships.

Recognizing that the implementation and scaling of the service are not happening quickly enough, deeply enough or with enough scale, Nyby is forging new paths. Nyby moved beyond the traditional categorization and relation between 'supplier and purchaser' to engage in deeper strategic partnerships with, as a start, the municipalities. This means they help develop the structures, the organizational setup, and anchor the necessary competencies within the organizations they collaborate with. According to founder Fredrik Gulowsen, this provides better conditions for accelerated implementation and scaling. In the current drafting of this text, Nyby collaborates with several Norwegian municipalities in exactly this way (Gulowsen, 2024).

Collaboration models for system change

We now readjust our gaze from the roles, characters and capabilities of societal change and zoom in on how collaboration among diverse stakeholder groups and roles can be orchestrated. Here, it is inspiring to look at the work of Hill, who in many ways has pioneered a design-driven and mission-oriented approach to system transformation, always with a focus on collaborative processes as well as place-based anchoring.

A vision for a city-scale biodiversity network

When we connected with Hill, he shared his latest work on the *Melbourne Biodiversity Network* (MBN) which, in many ways, serves as an inspiring example of how to co-create a shared strategic focus for solving a societal challenge, through the dedicated work of engaging a broad system of actors.

In his position as Director at Melbourne School of Design, Hill had collaborated with OFFICE, a not-for-profit multidisciplinary design and research practice in Melbourne and together had developed a strategic plan for unlocking biodiverse networks for community health and climate resilience (Melbourne Biodiversity Network, 2024). The plan proposes to build an interconnected network of public nature spaces that forms over 1,600 kilometres of biodiverse, ecological corridors across an area of 28,900 hectares. The strategy concludes the first two stages of a project that aims to recreate a city-scale network revealing, reconnecting, repairing and reproducing biodiversity spaces, woven into the contemporary city of Melbourne.

The background and the grand challenge for MBN is the dramatic decline of biodiversity in Australia that has the highest mammal extinction rate in the world. In the state of Victoria, over 50 per cent of the native vegetation has been cleared since the European settlement. Alongside this, climate change poses a continued and increasing threat to biodiversity, soil health, riverine flooding, sea level rises, increased urban heat and bushfires. The sum of these events makes the state of Victoria less resilient to the evermore frequent dramatic weather events caused by climate change.

The initiative sketched out by OFFICE and Hill is multipurposed, aiming to achieve both environmental and social benefits. First, by revegetating existing infrastructure corridors across the city of Melbourne, the aims are to rebuild biodiversity and ecosystem health and increase the city's resilience to climate change. Secondly, the project targets social benefits by encouraging more active, healthy and liveable communities through the development of new and accessible public green spaces, such as walking trails, bike paths and community spaces, along these corridors. As a third dimension, the project draws on the knowledge of First Peoples, utilizing approaches from Indigenous knowledge systems such as Care for Country; for example, by tracing songlines, the aboriginal walking routes and cultural landscapes that crossed the country, linking important sites, locations and bodies of knowledge.

The MBN Strategic Plan is a compelling visual document that aids the understanding of the potentials of the initiative. It visualizes 131 publicly owned corridors that are currently underutilized and undervalued. These are often former waterways, but now used simply as pipe tracks, chains of electricity pylons or retarding basins, for instance. The plan introduces ways of converting these corridors into treasured biodiversity corridors and sketches concrete, visual examples for restoring the infrastructure spaces into green communal areas, which distinctly redraws the map of Melbourne. Implementing the plan, implies establishing 1612 kilometres of possible biodiversity corridors all across Melbourne, which makes it one 'of the largest urban development projects in Australia' (Melbourne Biodiversity Network, 2024: 14).

To develop the MBN plan, the team has worked in a mission-oriented way and conducted a series of workshops and interviews with a broad and varied stakeholder group, including practitioners, researchers, local councils, state government agencies, volunteer groups and Traditional Owners. These groups helped define the purpose and potentials of the 131 corridors. Ultimately, 12 corridors were selected to serve as case studies for the coming two phases of the project that entails repairing and restoring the biodiversity corridors.

Nested governance

There are several inspiring approaches from the work behind the MBN project that we could point out. Hill is a frontrunner in his methodologically thorough approach to applying small-scale prototypes for the adaptive and modular spreading of city interventions. Yet, for the cause of this navigation point, we want to concentrate on Hill's *nested governance* model that cuts across different scales and system actors, recognizing that these systems are nested inside each other and that all stakeholders in their individual way, hold a shared responsibility for them:

> The job here is to hold many diverse agendas, to hold the big picture, because often those stakeholder groups have one or two or three agendas, but they may not have all of them. So, the state government sees the corridors as infrastructure just for carrying a pipe or something. The local group might see it as gardens or playgrounds or a nice place to grow fruit. The council, or the local industry might see it as something else. So, these approaches enable you to bring all those perspectives to the table around this idea of a multifaceted diverse view. (Hill, 2024a)

With the *nested governance* approach, Hill sets out to engage stakeholders at several city scales for multiple purposes yet insisting on how these different purposes and scales influence each other. The *place layers* diagram, Figure 9.2, visualizes the connections between the various city scales as well as their interconnectedness in the same shared system.

With this model as a visual point of reference, Hill can facilitate dialogue about the utilization of biodiversity corridors on the different scales in the city. In our view, here Hill takes on the role as a pathfinder who continuously zooms in and out of scales and points to the inherent connection between the different actors.

> When you put these diagrams in front of people, it lets them see how the scales are connected. The visual aid helps them conceptually recognize the value of

Figure 9.2: Place layers

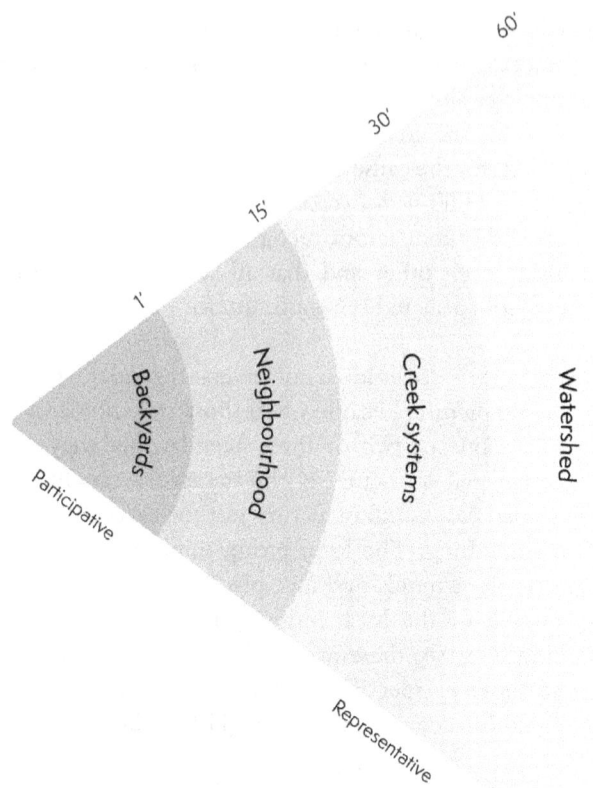

Note: Diagram of nested governance across the system allowing the approach to be reproduced at the scale of the city

Source: Dan Hill & Melbourne Biodiversity Network (Hill, 2024b)

thinking in this way. What you do at the backyard scale affects the watershed. If water becomes dirty at the backyard scale, it winds up dirty in the watershed. So, you have this systemic understanding of these things being connected. The neighbourhood system scale is sometimes really well handled by, for example, a land care group or a community organization. They can look after a creek. But it is very hard for a community organization to look after the whole watershed. That is usually where we have an Environmental Protection Agency or something like this. Yet equally it is very hard for an Environmental Protection Agency to look after your backyard. We need to think about how these scales can be joined together. (Hill, 2024a)

The nested governance model also recognizes that these different scales have different modes of engagement, where the local scale is highly participatory – you can quickly co-create local solutions around rehabilitating a local parkland. But participation in the regional grid is more representative, as development happens slowly over several years through large infrastructure planning.

Hill applies the nested governance model in different urban contexts such as energy grids, public transportation and the urban development of the streets of Stockholm. The principles behind the examples are the same. It helps us explore the interplay between community groups, schools, the municipality, the city infrastructure and so on, which Hill conceptualizes as 'place layers', derived from Stewart Brand's thinking around pace layers (Brand, 2018).

In this case, Hill's application of visual models lets the stakeholders understand how connected the entire corridor system is, and how dependent the different scales are on each other. This example underscores the valuable gains from utilizing design methods. A graphic visualization works as a point of reference and boundary object between stakeholders, hence, through the visual approach, Hill enables a different conversation and understanding of context and dependencies across local, regional and national levels.

The ownership struggle

Nested governance implies that we must work at different scales, and with different dynamics and ownership models at the same time. As we explored in *Navigating Balance*, once again, the pathfinder is back in the tense space between competing dynamics and attitudes. While Hill expressed to us that he increasingly meets more stakeholders who are willing to engage in these kinds of collaboration processes, it is clear that this model poses a real challenge to traditional ways of thinking about governance and collaboration.

We found this opinion to be seconded by another expert in urban planning, as we checked in with Christian Pagh, former director and chief curator of the Oslo Architecture Triennale and editor of the book *Mission Neighbourhood: (Re)Forming Communities*. From his experience with building neighbourhoods and local communities, Pagh highlighted the difficulties and tension between the neighbourhood scale and the city scale as well as their poor integration.

> It is a challenge linking the informal, spontaneous and socially dependent logics of local communities and neighbourhoods with the more formal structures of the municipality. The city administrations struggle to latch on to or benefit from the informal life and local potential in the city. The top-down, formal and risk-averse mechanics of the city administrations fail to connect with bottom-up and informal structures of the local scale. (Pagh, 2024)

One of the consequences of this lack of collaboration is an increase in what Pagh describes as 'boring and shallow' housing areas in newer residential developments.

The nested governance model and the way of thinking about interconnected systems and scales helps us provide a framework for stimulating mutual understanding and interactions between the different stakeholder groups. Yet, although this approach is powerful, it still leaves us with the question: Who is responsible for dealing with the problem and who takes responsibility for following through? Hill's role here is that of a transition broker, convening several stakeholders, working to adopt new ways into the system. But who anchors the projects in the system?

We posed these questions about ownership in societal change processes to Hill and his response was:

> Clearly, many of our challenges do not have a single owner. Take the climate crisis – who is the owner here? Who is the client for that task? There is no

client or simple ministerial relationship because these challenges are systemic and there is not a one-to-one mapping from problem to owner. So, what you need is an entity that can hold a system challenge without owning it and trying to influence it in some way. I try to find these kinds of hybrid positions or organizations that can hold that question. (Hill, 2024a)

The unique value of a project like MBN is how different groups of people come together around solving a joint challenge across stakeholder groups. Hill and OFFICE's external viewpoint, facilitation and processual skills are instrumental in scoping such a multipurpose systemic project. However, it is also a delicate setup, as the project is highly reliant on an external group to persistently build the momentum to create systemic change. This is a structural imbalance that we also experience in our work – staying outside of the institutional framework allows us to innovate, but challenges our ability to truly implement and anchor new structures.

This has made us continuously ask ourselves the nagging and somewhat pessimistic question: Are *any* institutions today capable of solving systemic problems? When we aired our reflection with Hill, he recognized this issue, stating: 'Institutions often do preserve the problem they are answering to. We could reframe how we think governance works to start working in the shape of the systems. But that's a really hard, long slog to do that' (Hill, 2024a).

That is why Hill seeks organizations that hold strong democratic legitimacy or seeks third spaces such as the Swedish government's innovation agency Vinnova or Finnish innovation fund Sitra that have an explicit mandate to drive innovation and systems change, because he recognizes that space to manoeuvre is more open.

Recomposing organizational structures

In the examples we bring forward that enable systemic change, we constantly see the appearance of *third spaces*: They either convene new types of collaboration, build new alliances or create new large initiatives that tap into and engage inside-outsiders.

The term *third spaces* originates from urban planning and the work of sociologist Ray Oldenburg and refers to a location that facilitates social interaction between people outside of the home sphere and work sphere. The concept highlights the influence and importance of third spaces for social cohesion, sense of belonging and civic engagement (Oldenburg, 1989).

We argue for an expanded interpretation of third spaces: seeing them as a space (not necessarily a physical or an organizational one) that opens between different key organizations and stakeholders engaged in solving a societal challenge. *Third spaces* free people from the confines of their organizations, its vested interests and ingrown structures, and lets them meet on equal terms where the shared goal or agenda is what drives them.

However, in our conversation with Hill, he insists we do not give up entirely on organizations and their ability to drive sustainable change:

> To counter the pessimism, it does not mean this is always going to be the case that organizations struggle to drive systems change. It is not a law of physics. It is not like we have to change gravity to fix how organizations work. It is a cultural pattern, behaviour or a political cultural framework, but it is not necessarily unchangeable. (Hill, 2024a)

Hill makes a direct link to the late anthropologist David Graeber, who challenged the notion that economic systems are natural or inevitable, arguing that, as human-made constructs, they can be reimagined or transformed. He puts emphasis on the idea that many aspects of our world are shaped by human actions and decisions rather than fixed laws or inherent qualities. Graeber's work is inspiring in its radical urge to challenge the status quo to recognize its power to reconfigure the world around them. If we can imagine something different, we can, in principle, design it.

Inspired by Graeber and Hill, it is alluring for the pathfinder to start testing and rehearsing how institutions and organizations can subtly begin to change, and how one can empower that change. This has been Hill's operating model for years, testing and playing with how to reconfigure organizational entities around a problem: for instance, with the mission he spearheaded with

Vinnova in Stockholm to *ensure that every street in Sweden is healthy, sustainable and vibrant by 2030*. The project team, comprising participants from all levels of government, industry stakeholders and community actors, in effect, rehearsed what it would be like to be a *street agency* – not a transportation agency, an environmental agency or a real estate agency, but an agency comprising all of these things, organized around creating healthy, sustainable and vibrant streets. This is where his ideas of nested governance and place layers were crystallized.

Recomposing an organization around the problem is also what we see unfold with the new Danish Ministry for the Green Tripartite Agreement. The resources and mandate are allocated around a cross-sectoral and interdisciplinary problem: the green transformation of the food and agricultural system. How this organizational setup will play out and how the power structures will evolve, is too soon to say. But it is promising to see a ministry designed around a challenge and its opportunities.

The optimistic notion that we can recompose organizations to wrap themselves around our challenges in new ways is encouraging. While the journey to change the entire makeup of our organizations is indeed long and bulky, there is a large potential for us to identify loopholes and pockets of change that allows us to reorganize ourselves around a challenge and its many opportunities. By doing so, we might build precedence for tomorrow's organizations.

What we have learned so far: navigating interdependence

In *Navigating Interdependence*, the theme of collaboration has been a consistent pulse.

We introduce the significance of bottom-up collaboration and cross-sectoral participation as a premise for successfully developing, initiating and magnifying societal change processes. Bottom-up collaboration is not only a premise for citizen engagement but a policy and business imperative.

To unfold these systems of diverse people and groups, we propose to (continuously) map the system in order to understand its inherent dynamics as well as to borrow from the participative practices of design.

We identify the pathfinder's role as an orchestrator or steward of a collaboration process that can simultaneously step back – leaving room for people to actively engage in and affect the process, while in synchrony maturing and amplifying a common shared direction.

There are key intermediary roles in the cast list for societal transition, such as transition brokers, inside-outsiders, entrepreneurs and retreaters, that we encourage scouting for and trying to engage in the most valuable ways. We introduce relevant capabilities from across society, highlighting the sometimes untapped potential of philanthropy, citizens and businesses.

For facilitating collaboration processes in practice, we bring forward the idea of nested governance and suggest working with visual aids to spur new dialogue and conversation across different layers of society.

We recognize that many institutions today struggle to be the drivers of societal change processes because of their embedded organizational interest. Here, we suggest working actively to reconfigure how organizations can be repurposed. As a last remark, we point to the power and potential of third spaces to assemble different groups around common societal challenges.

10

Closing and opening

Just before a star is born, there is total chaos.

It starts with a process of star formation in large cold interstellar clouds of gas and dust. Gravity pulls gas and dust together into dense cores, and the temperature and pressure starts to rise.

When the temperature reaches about 10 million degrees Celsius, nuclear fusion begins at the centre of the cloud, marking the birth of a star. The fusion converts hydrogen into helium, releasing enormous amounts of energy, and the star begins to emit light.

In this early phase, the star is called a protostar, and as it develops, it stabilizes as a main sequence star (*Scientific American*, 1999; NASA, 2024).

We started this book quoting Friedrich Nietzsche, 'One must still have chaos within oneself to give birth to a dancing star' (Nietzsche, 1977). Nietzsche's quote connects with the pathfinder's role and at times inner frustrating sentiment when navigating complexity and chaos to create new paths. The birth of a star stands as a testament to the image of transition we wish to leave you with as we conclude this book.

When we offer navigation points for pathfinders to lean on in the process of transition, we do know that this process is messy. It is confusing. And it is chaotic.

No matter how good a map we may provide, the pathfinder is left to make her own connections and conclusions. As Winhall suggests, the pathfinder must assess what is noise and what is signal, single out the signal and try to build momentum around it (Winhall, 2024).

This book invites you to make your own sense of the challenges and context you navigate, and to weigh up where and how you believe you can make the most significant difference. The four navigation points we present are large, perhaps overwhelming to some. We are not keen to promote the idea that one person in one job can or should be an expert in navigating all of them.

Thankfully, it is our experience that the world is full of pathfinders: innovative, curious and ambitious people, who are on the lookout for more to join them. We dream of you and many more convening, collaborating, uniting and helping each other out.

As we have been writing this book, the world has grown more fragmented and out of sync. Now, more than ever, it is essential that we weave a shared narrative in times marked by political division, disillusionment, mistrust, and deep fractures.

This book is an opener. It is not conclusive. It is merely one of many contributions to an exciting and emerging new practice and field. We, personally, are still on the journey and eager to learn more from people about how to navigate the chaos of societal change. The process of writing this book, of exploring with generous fellow thinkers and practitioners, has been a learning experience for us that we are hugely thankful for.

We hope that our reflections and experience have sparked ideas in your head and inspired new actions and conversations. That it has equipped you to embrace the chaos with courage, curiosity and a 'possibility thinking' mindset, believing that from this chaos, new stars can appear, and new constellations emerge.

Every second, 10 to 20 stars are born across all the galaxies in the universe. New stars can even materialize from the remnants of old stars when they die.

Acknowledgements and people to follow

We are deeply grateful to have learned and gained inspiration from influential, generous, charismatic thinkers and practitioners across different professional domains. They have helped shape our thinking and shed new light on our professional practice, inspiring ideas and perspectives through the book.

Christian Bason
PhD in design and leadership, former CEO of Danish Design Center and Mindlab, and author of several books on public sector innovation. Today, co-founder of Transition Collective, which drives cross-sector collaboration for innovation, transformation, and systemic change.

Bason is a close friend and former dear colleague with an insatiable thirst for learning and driving impact, especially in public sector innovation. He generously shares his knowledge and curiosity and has a formidable ability to see opportunities and pursue them in different pockets in society.

Dan Hill
Director of the Melbourne School of Design and Professor in Built Environment, Faculty of Architecture, Building and Planning, University of Melbourne. Dan previously led the strategic design function at Vinnova, the Swedish government's innovation agency, devising, prototyping and delivering mission-oriented innovation.

Hill is a global pioneer in systems design, urban planning and design-driven business. In all of his work, he brings a unique place-based approach to anchoring systems change in local and regional contexts. He elegantly illustrates and shares findings from his work through the development of visual models and new theories that broadly inspire change processes.

Geoff Mulgan
Professor of Collective Intelligence, Public Policy and Social Innovation at University College London (UCL). Former CEO of NESTA and visiting professor at UCL, the London School of Economics and the University of Melbourne. He has published several books on social innovation and imagination, policy

development and societal transformation, advising multiple organizations, including governments and foundations worldwide. He is currently an adviser to the European Parliament on science and technology.

Mulgan provokes and inspires societal transition work, offering a renewed perspective on the crucial role imagination plays in our society, both in the past, now and in the future. He connects the growth of society and policy making with art, creativity and design, providing a new language that actualizes design into other professional domains.

Ida Engholm

Design Professor at the Royal Danish Academy of Fine Arts, Schools of Architecture, Design and Conservation in Copenhagen.

Engholm's work reveals an infectious curiosity and high expectations for design's transformative role today and in the future. Her experimental mindset and critical ideas draw beautiful connections across the corners of society, from history to religion, philosophy, economics, design and organizational theory.

Jacqueline Cramer

Sustainability change maker, Emeritus Professor and former Cabinet Minister of Housing, Spatial Planning and Environment in the Netherlands.

Cramer is a pioneer of the circular transition in the Netherlands. She is a multifaceted and brave character with ties to industry, research and non-governmental organizations, and she energetically brings these worlds together as she builds up coalitions of change.

Jennie Winhall

Social Innovator and Designer, Founder of System Shift and Founder and Director of ALT/Now, a system innovation agency. Jennie has pioneered and developed multiple frameworks and perspectives on system innovation from her profound experience over the last two decades, working with governments, municipalities, foundations, and businesses to create a more significant systemic impact on social challenges.

Together with her fellow thinker Charles Leadbeater, Winhall has an admirably deep curiosity in understanding drivers, conditions and people that shape our systems. She masters a superior level of reflection, which means she can find meaning in chaos and provide models and approaches others can find helpful in their transition work.

Rowan Conway
Deputy Director at the Just Transition Finance Lab and Visiting Professor of Practice, UCL's Institute of Innovation and Public Purpose.

Conway impressively combines design, research, political theory and system innovation often in the context of mission-oriented innovation. She is impressive in how she critically, relentlessly and creatively unpacks how the government and policy can work to drive real transformation.

Søren Vester Haldrup
Today Søren Vester Haldrup works with Transnational Corruption and Financial Integrity at the United Nations Development Programme (UNDP) bringing a systems perspective to a complex societal challenge. Previously, Haldrup was Innovation Fund Manager and head of the Measuring and Evaluation (M&E) Sandbox at UNDP.

Haldrup has been a global pioneer in rethinking impact measurement and evaluation building a thriving community of over 200 organizations that share learning on innovative M&E. In this role, he has generously shared his findings and insights openly from this work through global events and communication, encouraging many more to join the movement.

Furthermore, we would like to thank a group of inspiring people who have generously made their knowledge available and shared their experience: Joana Sá Lima Skrede, Halvor Skrede, Tobias Revell, Jesper Christiansen, Jakob Schjørring, Mikkel Holst, Jon Alexander, Oskar Stokholm Østergaard, Rainer Kattel, Mette Elf, Piret Tõnurist, Alexander Holt, Christian Pagh, Brian Frandsen, Fredrik Gulowsen and Martin S. Hansen.

Finally, a special thanks to My Buemann for the illustrations that bring this book to life.

References

Alexander, J. (2024) Interview, online, September.

American Accounting Association (2018) 'In What They Believe a First', https://aaahq.org/Outreach/Newsroom/Press-Releases/1-22-18-In-what-they-believe-a-first [Accessed 12 August 2024].

Austin, R. and Bason, C. (2019) 'The Right Way to Lead Design Thinking', *Harvard Business Review*, https://hbr.org/2019/03/the-right-way-to-lead-design-thinking [Accessed 14 April 2025].

Bason, C. (2010) *Leading Public Sector Innovation: Co-creating for a Better Society*, Policy Press.

Bason, C. (2016) *Design for Policy*, Routledge.

Bason, C. (2024) Interview, online, August.

Bason, C. and Skibsted, J.M. (2022) *Expand: Stretching the Future by Design*, BenBella Books.

Bason, C. and Striegler, S. (2023) 'Design af missionsorienteret innovation – en ny vej for mental trivsel', in Winther Nielsen, S. (ed) *Vilde Problemer*, Nord Academic, pp 190–216.

Benyus, M.J. (2002) *Biomimicry Innovation Inspired by Nature*, Harper Collins.

Bertermann, K. and Coffman, J. (2024) 'Embedding Learning in Systems Change', *Center for Evaluation Innovation*, https://evaluationinnovation.org/publication/a-framework-for-embedding-learning-in-systems-change/ [Accessed 18 February 2025].

Brand, S. (2018) 'Pace Layering: How Complex Systems Learn and Keep Learning', *Journal of Design and Science*. https://doi.org/10.21428/7f2e5f08

Brown, B. (2018) *Dare to Lead – Brave Work. Tough Conversations. Whole Hearts*, Random House.

References

Brown, T. (2009) *Change by Design*, HarperCollins.

Conway, R. (2024a) Interview, online, June.

Conway, R. (2024b) 'Designing Transformation', public talk, *IIPP Forum 2024*, https://www.ucl.ac.uk/bartlett/public-purpose/events/2024/jun/designing-transformation [Accessed 9 October 2024].

Conway, R. and Massey-Brooker, A. (2024) 'Mission-oriented Innovation for Sustainable Polymers in Liquid Formulation', *Philosophical Transactions*, https://royalsocietypublishing.org/doi/10.1098/rsta.2023.0272 [Accessed 25 September 2024].

Conway, R., Leadbeater, C. and Winhall, J. (2019) 'The Impact Entrepreneur: Building a New Platform for Economic Security in Work', *Royal Society for the Encouragement of Arts, Manufactures and Commerce*, https://www.thersa.org/reports/impact-entrepreneur-economic-security-work/ [Accessed 4 October 2024].

Cramer, J. (2020) *How Network Governance Powers the Circular Economy: Ten Guiding Principles for Building a Circular Economy, Based on Dutch Experiences*, Amsterdam Economic Board.

Cramer, J. (2024) Interview, online, August.

Danmarks Radio (2023) 'Medieudvklingen 2022: Fri os fra nyhederne', *Danmarks Radio*, https://www.dr.dk/om-dr/fakta-om-dr/medieforskning/medieudviklingen/2022/fri-os-fra-nyhederne [Accessed 27 October 2024].

DDC (Danish Design Center) (2018a) 'Boxing Future Health: Enacting Alternative Futures as a Trigger for Change', *DDC*, https://ddc.dk/cases/boxing-future-health/ [Accessed 31 October 2024].

DDC (2018b) 'Boxing Future Health: På besøg i fremtidens sundhed 2050', *DDC*, https://ddc.dk/wp-content/uploads/2021/12/Feltbog_Boxing.pdf [Accessed 21 February 2025].

DDC (2018c) 'Boxing Future Health'. Excerpt from workshop material, audio file, http://boxingfuturehealth.dk/en/ [Accessed 14 April 2025].

DDC (2018d) 'Co-creating the Future with University College Copenhagen', *DDC*, https://ddc.dk/cases/co-creating-the-future/ [Accessed 17 October 2024].

DDC (2020) 'Living Futures: Scenario Kit', *DDC*, https://living futures.org/ [Accessed 31 October 2024].

DDC (2021) 'Mission Playbook 1.0: A Design-driven Approach to Launching and Driving Missions', *DDC*, https://ddc.dk/tools/missions-playbook-a-design-driven-approach-to-launching-and-driving-missions/ [Accessed 4 October 2024].

DDC and Kolding Municipality (2023) Unpublished data from a collaboration between DDC and Kolding Municipality.

Dengsøe, I. (2024) 'Nogle gange er det bedste, vi kan gøre for patienterne, faktisk ingenting', *The Region of Southern Denmark*, https://regionsyddanmark.dk/om-region-syddanmark/presse-og-nyheder/magasinet-sund-i-syd/tema-om-fremtidens-sundhedsvaesen/nogle-gange-er-det-bedste-vi-kan-gore-for-patienterne-faktisk-ingenting [Accessed 23 October 2024].

Design Council (2004) 'The Double Diamond', *Design Council*, https://www.designcouncil.org.uk/our-resources/the-double-diamond/ [Accessed 17 September 2024].

Dorst, K. (2011) *The Core of 'Design Thinking' and its Application*, Design Studies.

Dunne, A. and Raby, F. (2013) *Speculative Everything: Design, Fiction, and Social Dreaming*, MIT Press.

Edmondson, A. (1999) 'Psychological Safety and Learning Behaviour in Work Teams', *Administrative Science Quarterly*, 44(2): 350–383.

Edmondson, A. (2018) *The Fearless Organization: Creating Psychological Safety in the Workplace for Learning, Innovation, and Growth*, Wiley Publishing.

Edmondson, A.C. (2023) *Right Kind of Wrong: The Science of Failing Well*, Cornerstone.

Elf, M.M. (2024) Interview, online, September.

Engholm, I. (2023) *Design for the New World: From Human Design to Planet Design*, Intellect Books.

Eno, B. (2009) 'More dark than shark – feature', interview at Luminous Sydney Festival, *More Dark than Shark*, https://www.moredarkthanshark.org/feature_luminous2.html [Accessed 15 August 2024].

Esbjørnsen, A. and Normann, E. (2024) 'Få danskere tror på, at politikernes forslag kan føres ud i livet. Nu kommer en mulig løsning', *Zetland*, https://www.zetland.dk/historie/seg65q9l-m8yvvdRQ-7d4df [Accessed 31 October 2024].

References

European Commission Joint Research Centre (2018) 'Facts4EUFuture: A Series of Reports for the Future of Europe', *EU Science Hub*, https://joint-research-centre.ec.europa.eu/jrc-mission-statement-work-programme/facts4eufuture_en [Accessed 18 October 2024].

The Fifth Dimension (2023) 'Embracing Playful Seriousness and Serious Playfulness', *Medium*, https://medium.com/@nickbeats1454/embracing-playful-seriousness-and-serious-playfulness-1902ea926879, https://en.wikipedia.org/wiki/Serious_play [Accessed 24 June 2024].

Frandsen, B. (2024) Interview, Copenhagen, August.

Fry, T. (2007) 'Redirective Practices: An Elaboration', *Design Philosophy Papers*, 5(1): 5–20.

Future Generations Commissioner of Wales (2015) 'Well-being of Future Generations (Wales) Act', *Future Generations Commissioner of Wales*, https://www.futuregenerations.wales/about-us/future-generations-act/ [Accessed 19 September 2024].

Graeber, D. (2016) *The Utopia of Rules: On Technology, Stupidity, and the Secret Joys of Bureaucracy*, Melville House Publishing.

Gronchi, I. (2023) Interview, online, December.

Gulowsen, F. (2024) Interview, online, June.

Haldrup, S.V. (2023) 'How to Track and Report on Progress when Working with Complex Problems', *Medium*, https://medium.com/@undp.innovation/how-to-track-and-report-on-progress-when-working-with-complex-problems-28249a2bab87 [Accessed 11 October 2024].

Haldrup, S.V. (2024) Interview, online, October.

Harrabin, R. (2021) 'Climate Change: Young People Very Worried', *BBC*, https://www.bbc.com/news/world-58549373 [Accessed 27 October 2024].

Hebsgaard, T. (2024) 'Er vi tæt på et historisk øjeblik, der kan redde naturen?', *Zetland*, https://www.zetland.dk/historie/sevgaxqg-m8yvvdRQ-38aa9 [Accessed 4 October 2024].

Heshmat, S. (2022) '5 Benefits of Imaginative Thinking', *Psychology Today*, https://www.psychologytoday.com/us/blog/science-choice/202204/5-benefits-imaginative-thinking [Accessed 16 September 2024].

Hill, D. (2024a) Interview, online, August.

Hill, D. (2024b) 'Unlocking Biodiverse Networks for Community Health and Climate Resilience: Strategic Plan 2024', *OFFICE & University of Melbourne*, https://office.org.au/api/wp-content/uploads/2024/08/OFFICE_UoM_Melbourne-Biodiversity-Network.pdf [Accessed 29 October 2024].

Hill, D. and Melander, A. (2025) 'Strategic Design for Public Purpose: Enriched and Expanded Practices for Human-technology Interaction', in Malakhatka, E. and Wiberg, M. (eds) *Human-Technology Interaction*, Springer, pp 23–80.

Hill, D. and Vinnova (2022) *Designing Missions: Mission-oriented Innovation in Sweden. A Practice Guide by Vinnova*, Vinnova.

Holst, M. (2024) Interview, Copenhagen, August.

Holten, E. (2024) *Underskud*, Politikens Forlag.

Hopkins, R. (2019) 'The Importance of Imagination: An Interview with Rob Hopkins', *Resilience*, https://www.resilience.org/stories/2019-11-19/the-importance-of-imagination-an-interview-with-rob-hopkins/ [Accessed 27 October 2024].

Hopkins, R. (2020) *From What Is to What If: Unleashing the Power of Imagination to Create the Future We Want*, Chelsea Green Publishing Company.

Huizinga, J. (1938) *Homo Ludens: A Study of the Play-Element in Culture*, Beacon Press.

Indigenous People (2016) 'Constitution of the Iroquois Nations: The Great Binding Law', *Indigenous People*, https://www.indigenouspeople.net/iroqcon.htm [Accessed 19 September 2024].

Irwin T., Gideon, T. and Tonkinwise, C. (2015) 'Transition Design Provocation', *Design Philosophy Papers*, 13(1): 3–11. DOI: 10.1080/14487136.2015.1085688

Iskander, N. (2018) 'Design Thinking Is Fundamentally Conservative and Preserves the Status Quo', *Harvard Business Review*, https://hbr.org/2018/09/design-thinking-is-fundamentally-conservative-and-preserves-the-status-quo [Accessed 13 August 2024].

Jameson, F. (2003) 'Future City', *New Left Review*, 21: 65-79.

Kahn, J. (2022) 'Brian Eno Explains the Beautiful Benefits of Singing', *Farout Magazine*, May, https://faroutmagazine.co.uk/brian-eno-beautiful-benefits-of-singing/ [Accessed 24 August 2024].

References

Kattel, R. (2023) 'Dynamic Evaluation: Theory Meets Practice', public event, *Moin Global Gathering*, 7 June, https://www.ucl.ac.uk/bartlett/public-purpose/events/2023/jun/dynamic-evaluation-theory-meets-practice [Accessed 28 January 2025].

Kierkegaard, S. (1849) Sygdommen til Døden. En christelig psychologisk Udvikling til Opbyggelse og Opvækkelse af Anti-Climacus. CA Reitzel, vol 11.

Kimbell, L. and Vesnic-Alujevic, L. (2020) 'After the Toolkit: Anticipatory Logics and the Future of Government', *Policy Design and Practice*, 3(2): 95–108. https://doi.org/10.1080/25741292.2020.1763545

Kongstad, M. (2024) 'Vi er nødt til at gøre klimakampen mere sexet', *Zetland*, https://www.zetland.dk/historie/soGxZDVN-m8yvvdRQ-78905 [Accessed 25 September 2024].

KS (2022) 'Fra Ungdom til Ung Voksen', *KS*, https://www.ks.no/fagomrader/innovasjon/partnerskap-for-radikal-innovasjon/ungt-utenforskap/fra-ungdom-til-ung-voksen/ [Accessed 27 October 2024].

Laloux, F. (2014) *Reinventing Organisations: A Guide to Creating Organizations Inspired by the Next Stage in Human Consciousness*, Nelson Parker.

Larsen, J.A. and Hansen, L.B. (2022) 'Disse emner er de vigtigste for danskerne under valgkampen vurderer eksperter', *Folketingsvalg 2022*, TV2, https://nyheder.tv2.dk/politik/2022-07-30-sundhed-er-vigtigst-for-danskerne-til-det-kommende-valg-viser-ny-maaling [Accessed 17 September 2024].

Larsen, A.F., Bjerge, B. and Brendstrup, S. (2024) 'Impact Framework for Mission-oriented Innovation', *Innovation Fund Denmark*.

Latour, B. (2007) *Reassembling the Social: An Introduction to Actor-Network-Theory*, Oxford University Press.

Latour, B. and Schultz, N. (2022) *On the Emergence of the Ecological Class: A Memo*, Polity.

Leadbeater, C. and Winhall, J. (2020) 'Building Better Systems: A Green Paper on System Innovation', *The Rockwool Foundation*.

Leadbeater, C. and Winhall, J. (2021) 'The Power to Shift a System', *System Shift Initiative, The Rockwool Foundation*

Lima, J.S. (2024) Interview, online, May.

Lyngaae, U. (2024) Har fyret mig selv som chef, *Linkedin*, https://www.linkedin.com/feed/update/urn:li:activity:7228769015563751424/ [Accessed 29 September 2024].

Mannervik, U. and Ramirez, R. (2016) *Strategy for a Networked World*, Imperial College Press.

Manzini, M. (2015) *Design, When Everybody Designs: An Introduction to Design for Social Innovation*, MIT Press.

Mazzucato, M. (2018a) *The Entrepreneurial State*, Penguin Books.

Mazzucato, M. (2018b) 'Mission-oriented Research & Innovation in the European Union', *European Commission*.

Mazzucato, M. (2021) *Mission Economy: A Moonshot Guide to Changing Capitalism*, Penguin Books.

McKinsey & Company (2022) 'The State of Fashion 2022', *McKinsey & Company*.

Meadows, D. (1999) 'Leverage Points: Places to Intervene in a System', *The Sustainability Institute*.

Meadows, D. (2008) *Thinking In Systems: A Primer*, Chelsea Green Publishing.

Melbourne Biodiversity Network (2024) 'Unlocking Biodiverse Networks for Community Health and Climate Resilience: Strategic Plan 2024', *OFFICE & University of Melbourne*, https://office.org.au/api/wp-content/uploads/2024/08/OFFICE_UoM_Melbourne-Biodiversity-Network.pdf [Accessed 29 October 2024].

Merriam Webster Dictionary (nd) 'Definition of Experiment', https://www.merriam-webster.com/dictionary/experiment [Accessed 31 October 2024].

Mulgan, G. (2020) 'The Imaginary Crisis (and How We Might Quicken Social and Public Imagination)', *UCL, Demos Helsinki and Untitled*.

Mulgan, G. (2022) *Another World is Possible*, C Hurst & Co Publishers Ltd.

Muratovski, G. (2023) 'In Conversation with Ezio Manzini: Design for Social Innovation – What We've Learned So Far', *The Journal of Design, Economics, and Innovation*, 9(1). https://doi.org/10.1016/j.sheji.2022.12.003

Myers, W. (2014) *Bio Design, Nature – Science – Creativity*, Thames and Hudson.

References

NASA (National Aeronautics and Space Administration) (2024) 'Star Basics', *NASA*, https://science.nasa.gov/universe/stars/ [Accessed 20 February 2025].

Nelson, R. (1977) *The Moon and the Ghetto*, W.W. Norton & Co.

Nietzsche, F. (1977) *Thus Spoke Zarathustra: A Book for All and None*, translated by R.J. Hollingdale, Penguin Classics.

Nyby (2024) 'Sammen skaber vi morgendagens velfærdssamfund', *Nyby*, https://dk.nyby.com/ [Accessed 26 October 2024].

OECD (Organisation for Economic Co-operation and Development) (2019) 'Anticipatory Governance', *OECD*, https://www.oecd.org/en/topics/anticipatory-governance.html [Accessed 18 October 2024].

OECD (2022) 'Tackling Policy Challenges Through Public Sector Innovation: A Strategic Portfolio Approach', *OECD Public Governance Reviews*, OECD Publishing. https://doi.org/10.1787/052b06b7-en

Oldenburg, R. (1989) *Great Good Place*, Da Capo Press.

Østergaard, O.S. (2024a) Interview, Copenhagen, September.

Østergaard, O.S. (2024b) 'Mission Playbook, 5 Reflections Letting the Imagination Bloom for Design-Driven Missions', *DDC*, https://ddc.dk/tools/mission-playbook-design-driven-approach-to-launching-and-driving-missions/ [Accessed 27 October 2024].

Østergaard, O.S., Striegler, S. and Erlendsson, A. (2023) 'Alternative Futures Can Give Us New Perspectives on the Wicked Problems of the Present', *Wicked Series, DDC*, https://ddc.dk/wp-content/uploads/2023/12/Wicked-Series-The-Collection.pdf [Accessed 16 September 2024].

Pagh, C. (2024) Interview, online, August.

Panduro, J. (2023) Interview, Copenhagen, October.

Pedersen, D.M.B. (2024) *Mission Guidebook: A Research Management Guide to Mission-driven Universities*, Aalborg University.

Pink, D. (2018) *Drive: The Truth About What Motivates Us*, Canongate Books.

Polchar, J. (2021) Conversation with Joshua Polchar, strategic foresight lead at OPSI, OECD.

Poulman, P (2021) *Net Positive – How courageous companies thrive by giving more than they take* Harward Business Review Press.

Prime Minister's Office (2020) 'Press Conference on COVID-19', speech by Prime Minister Mette Frederiksen, https://www.stm.dk/presse/pressemoedearkiv/pressemoede-om-covid-19-den-11-marts-2020/ [Accessed 6 September 2024].

Project Hestia (2016) 'Hestia: A Comparative Multi-site Study', Hestia Research Project, https://www.projecthestia.com/en/about/ [Accessed 11 August 2024].

Ramirez, R. and Wilkinson, A. (2016) *Strategic Reframing: The Oxford Scenario Planning Approach*, Oxford University Press.

Raupp, J. (2022) '"The Situation Is Serious": Angela Merkel's Crisis Communication in the COVID-19 Pandemic', in Maarek, P.J. (ed) *Manufacturing Government Communication on Covid-19*, Springer.

Realdania (2022) 'Fremtidens Bæredygtige Landskaber', *Realdania*, https://realdania.dk/projekter/fremtidens-b%C3%A6redygtige-landskaber [Accessed 22 October 2024].

Realdania (2023) 'Seven Danish Initiatives Inspired by Collective Impact 2014–2022: A Collection of Case Stories', https://realdania.dk/publikationer/faglige-publikationer/seven-danish-initiatives-inspired-by-collective-impact-2014-2022 [Accessed 29 October 2024].

Rittel, H. and Webber, M.M. (1973) *Dilemmas in a General Theory of Planning*, Policy Sciences.

Robertson, B.J. (2016) *Holacracy: The Revolutionary Management System that Abolishes Hierarchy*, Penguin Books.

Royal Chemistry Society (2023) 'The PLFs Revolution: Our 2040 Roadmap for Sustainable Polymers in Liquid Formulations', *Royal Chemistry Society*, https://online.flippingbook.com/view/12956728/20/ [Accessed 20 August 2024].

Sandborg, L. (2023) 'Nye tal: Hver fjerde unge kvinde overvejer ikke at få børn grundet klimaforandringer', *Information*, https://www.information.dk/indland/2023/04/nye-tal-hver-fjerde-unge-kvinde-overvejer-faa-boern-grundet-klimaforandringer [Accessed 27 October 2024].

Schilhab, T., Juelskjær, M. and Moser, T. (2008) *Learning Bodies*, Danmarks Pædagogiske Universitetsforlag.

Schjørring, J. (2025) Interview, online, January.

Scientific American (1999) 'How is a star born?', *Scientific American*, https://www.scientificamerican.com/article/how-is-a-star-born/ [Accessed 26 February 2025].

References

Selin, C. (2021) Scenario Planning and Foresight from Oxford University and Saïd Business School [lecture in course on Scenario Planning at Oxford University].

Senge, P. (2006) *The Fifth Discipline: The Art & Practice of the Learning Organization*, Doubleday.

Sharpe, B. (2020) *The Three Horizons: The Patterning of Hope*, International Futures Forum and Triarchy Press.

Simon, H. (1969) *The Sciences of the Artificial*, The MIT Press.

Sinek, S. (2019) *Start With Why: How Great Leaders Inspire Everyone to Take Action*, Penguin Books.

Star, S.L. and Griesemer, J.R. (1989) *Institutional Ecology, 'Translations' and Boundary Objects: Amateurs and Professionals in Berkeley's Museum of Vertebrate Zoology*, Social Studies of Science.

State of Green (2024) 'Denmark Announces Historic Tripartite Agreement to Cut Agricultural Carbon Emissions and Restore Nature', *State of Green*, https://stateofgreen.com/en/news/denmark-announces-historic-tripartite-agreement-to-cut-agricultural-carbon-emissions-and-restore-nature/ [Accessed 2 October 2024].

Striegler, S. and Buhelt, A. (2023) 'Stretching Our Empathy to Future Generations', *DDC* [originally published in Danish in *Impact Insider*], https://ddc.dk/stretching-our-empathy-to-future-generations/ [Accessed 8 August 2024].

Striegler, S. and Erlendsson, A. (2023) 'How to Turn Wicked Problems Into Ambitious Opportunities', in *Wicked Series, DDC*, https://ddc.dk/wp-content/uploads/2023/12/Wicked-Series-The-Collection.pdf [Accessed 20 September 2024].

Striegler, S., Ørnsholt, S.S. and Erlendsson, A. (2023) 'Missioner viser vej til handling i vildnisset af komplekse problemer', *Impact Insider*, https://impactinsider.dk/kronik-missioner-viser-vej-til-handling-i-vildnisset-af-komplekse-problemer/ [Accessed 31 October 2024].

Superflux (2021) 'Refuge for Resurgence', Exhibition at Biennale Architettura, *La Biennale di Venezia*, https://superflux.in/index.php/work/refuge-for-resurgence/# [Accessed 31 October 2024].

Sydendal, E. (2024) Inspirational speech at Open Academy, Academy for Social Innovation, Copenhagen, 5 September.

Tech BBQ (2024) 'Denmark is Taking Steps to be in the Forefront of the Life Science Industry', panel debate, *Tech BBQ*.

Thurfjell, K. (2020) 'New Nordic Cuisine is the New Normal', *Nordic Co-operation, The Nordic Council and the Nordic Council of Ministers*, https://www.norden.org/en/information/new-nordic-cuisine-new-normal [Accessed 4 September 2024].

Tõnurist, P. (2023) '13 Reasons Why Missions Fail', *OPSI Observatory of Public Sector Innovation*, https://doi.org/10.1787/052b06b7-en [Accessed 8 August 2024].

Tõnurist, P. (2024) Interview, online, June.

Trebeck, K. and Smith, W. (2024) 'The Wellbeing Economy in Brief: Understanding the Growing Agenda and its Implications', *Centre for Policy Development*.

Vervoort, J. (2022) 'Deep Seriousness and Deep Playfulness are not Opposites', *Medium*, https://anticiplay.medium.com/deep-seriousness-and-deep-playfulness-are-not-opposites-c57ee718105 [Accessed 24 June 2024].

Vind, D.L. (2024) 'Circular Economy', *Way of Life*, https://wayoflifenow.com/circular-economy/ [Accessed 14 August 2024].

Vinnova (2021) 'The Street as a Meeting Place Instead of a Parking Lot', *Vinnova*, https://www.vinnova.se/en/news/2021/03/the-street-as-a-meeting-place-instead-of-a-parking-lot/ [Accessed 14 August 2024].

Wadhwani, T. (2022) 'Reflections from Circular Economy Expert Professor Jacqueline Cramer's Australian Visit', *Australian Circular Economy Hub*, https://acehub.org.au/news/reflections-from-circular-economy-expert-professor-jacqueline-cramers [Accessed 20 August 2024].

Winhall, J. (2024) Interview, online, September.

Winther Nielsen, S. (2023) *Vilde problemer – Værktøjskasse til politikere, praktikere og policy-entreprenører*, Nord Academic.

World Health Organization (2016) 'Global Strategy on Human Resources for Health: Workforce 2030', *World Health Organization*, https://iris.who.int/bitstream/handle/10665/250368/9789241511131-eng.pdf [Accessed 17 September 2024].

The authors utilised Chat GPT as an expanded search engine beyond Google for initial research, and in some cases to translate words from Danish to English. Any information provided by ChatGPT was personally checked by a human to ensure accuracy.

Index

References to figures appear in *italic* type; those in **bold** type refer to tables.

A

abductive reasoning 101–102
Actor Network Theory (ANT) 13, 144
adaptive portfolios 82–85
agricultural system reform 162–164
Alexander, Jon 77, 165
anxiety 18, 19, 20, 48
Austin, Robert 130
Australia
  Drought Resilience mission 75
  Melbourne Biodiversity Network (MBN) 167–173

B

backcasting 86–88
Bason, Christian 47, 48, 63, 67, 79, 82, 111, 130, 148, 165–166, 179
Benyus, Janine M. 141
Bertermann, K. 125, *126*
Bikuben Foundation 117–118, 122
biodiversity networks 167–173
body vs. life 37
boundary objects 42, 48
Boxing Future Health 36–44, 52, 102
  anchoring scenarios in healthcare sector 42–43
  immersion in alternative futures 41–42
  matrix *37*
  notion of health and disease 37
  organization of healthcare 37–38
businesses, capacity to contribute for societal change 165–167

C

cancer mission, European Union 75
Candy, Stuart 52

capabilities in societal transition 162–167
capitalism 30–31
Child's Law 123
Choose Wisely project 72
Christiania, Copenhagen 150–152, 159
circular transitions 142–143, 153–155
  concrete industry 154, 156
  mapping and analysing 144
  PLFs 86
citizens, active 165
climate change 19, 22, 59, 100
  Climate Act to tackle 157
  dominant narrative around 32
  failure to act on 67–68
  MBN and increasing resilience to 167–168
  ownership of 172–173
  willingness to act on 31–32
co-creation 148, 149
CO_2 emissions
  documenting 143
  law for reduction in 157
coalition building 153–176
  cast list for systems change 158–162
  collaboration models for system change 167–173
  need for multiple capabilities 162–167
  power of intermediaries 157–158
  recomposing organizational structures 173–175
coalition of the willing 153–154
Coffman, J. 125, *126*
cognitive leap 100–103
collaboration 139–152, 175–176
  driving collaboration through design 147–149

learning from ecosystems 141–143
mapping and analysing
    systems 144–147
releasing control 150–152
collaboration models for system
    change 167–173
  nested governance 169–171,
    170, 175
  ownership struggle 171–173
  vision for a city-scale biodiversity
    network 167–168
collective mindset
  leading collective change
    processes 131–133
  unlocking 129–130
company reporting 68–69
Comte Bureau 110–111,
    112–113, 125
Concrete Agreement 154, 156
conductor, steward and
    shepherd 149–150
connectors and conveners 65
control, releasing 150–152
convergent thinking 63
Conway, Rowan *78*, 86–88,
    100, 181
COVID-19 crisis 21, 30, 95–96,
    98, 99
Cramer, Jacqueline 153–156,
    157–158, 180
creativity 20, 32, 62
crises, recent 21–22

D

Danish Design Center (DDC). 3, 7,
    8, 18, 36, *38*, 42, 47, 48, 79, 83,
    101, 103, 133, 143
Danish National Health Profile,
    2021 47–48
Decoupling 2030 82–85
design 1, 2–6
  broad range of disciplines 3, *4*
  connecting to
    theoretical domains 6
  core characteristics 3–5
  -led missions 8
  thinking 63
Design Council, UK 63, 64, *65*
designers 5
  four roles for 64–65
  and makers 65
directionality 46, 74–75, 82
divergent thinking 63

double diamond model 63–64, *64*
Drought Resilience mission 75
Dunne, Anthony 9
dynamic learning in political
    decision making 127–129

E

ecological class 31
ecology 31–32
ecosystems, learning from 141–143
Edmondson, Amy C. 99–100,
    107–108
educational system 20
electric cars 91–92
Elf, Mette Margrethe 163
enablers of change 92
Engholm, Ida xii, 3, 25, 30,
    61, 63, 66, 67, 89, 102,
    114, 180
Eno, Brian 137, 139
entrepreneurial states 6
entrepreneurs 159, 160
ESG – Environmental, Social and
    Governance reporting 143
European Commission Joint
    Research Centre 10
European Union missions 7, 75
experiments 97–108
  cognitive leap 100–103
  daring to question 107–108
  defining 98–99
  elements interacting in loops 109
  harvesting learning from
    119–122, *121*
  portfolio of 113–114
  preparation 99–100
  resistance to 99
  staying serious yet playful 103–107
  towards preferred future 100, 118

F

fashion, trends in 59–60
feedback loops 11–12, 26
Finland, Committee on the
    Future 10, 69
followership 13–14, 133
foster care to adulthood,
    transitioning from 116–119
  harvesting learning across
    portfolios 122
  harvesting learning from
    experiments 119–122, *121*
  system level learning 122–123

Index

Four Keys 12, 26–28
  in practice 28–29
Frandsen, Brian 62
Frederiksen, Mette 95
Future Committees 10, 69
future generations 20, 51, 67, 68, 69
Future Generations Commissioner, Wales 69
futures design 2, 8–10, 45–46
  connection to system innovation 29
  expanding our perspective through 34–35
  integrating imagination and 51–52
  future scenarios 38–41

G

gender equality 70–71
governance models, changing 82–85
Graeber, David 46, 174
Green Tripartite Agreement 162–164, 175
Gronchi, Iacopo 132

H

Haldrup, Søren Vester 124–127, 181
Harvesting Learning Model 115–116, *116*, 125
  learning across portfolios 122
  learning from experiments 119–122
  system level learning 122–123
Haudenosaunee Confederacy 68
health bazaar 39–41
healthcare
  assistants' recruitment crisis x–xi
  Choose Wisely project 72
healthcare, unlocking system of Danish 35–44
  Boxing Future Health 36–42
  anchoring scenarios in healthcare sector 42–43
  future scenarios 38–41
  immersion in alternative futures 41–42
  matrix 37
  notion of health and disease 37
  organization of healthcare 37–38
  reflections on recommendations for reform 43–44
Hestia project 28–29
high amplitude thinking 61–62
Hill, Dan 137, 144, 149, 167, 169–171, 172–173, 174, 179

Holst, Mikkel 150–152, 159
Holten, Emma 34
Hopkins, Rob 18, 20, 32, 104
Horizon Europe 7
Huizinga, Johan 104
human needs, design for 148
hypothesis, learning through 109–135
  creating an hypothesis 109–110
  dynamic learning in political decision making 127–129
  learning at different scales 115–123
  learning forward 114–115
  measuring impact 123–127
  moving to a different kind of leadership 129–133
  new organizational shapes 133–134
  prototyping 111–114
  reducing loneliness among young students 110–111, 112–113

I

imagination crisis 17–44
  appetite for new approaches 23–25
  changing the systems 25–29
  in an era of opportunities 29–30
  expanding our perspective through futures design 34–35
  faltering ability to reimagine 18–19
  igniting hope and agency 30–34
  lacking incentives and structures 19–21
  reasons to care about 18–19
  unknown yet predictable future 21–23
  unlocking system of healthcare 35–44
Impact Framework for Mission-oriented Innovation 90–92, *90*, 124
impatient and patient mindsets 60
Indigenous
  knowledge systems 168
  'seven generation principle' 68
Innovation Fund Denmark 90, *90*
innovators, stakeholder group 155–156
inside-outsiders 159–160, *160*
Intergovernmental Panel on Climate Change 68
INVI 127–129

J

Jameson, Frederic 30

K

Kattel, Rainer 123
key performance indicators (KPIs) 117, 123, 131, 132
Kirkegaard, Søren xiii
Kongstad, Martin 31–32

L

Laloux, Frederic 12–13, 133
land use reform 162–164
Larsen, J. A. 35, 90
Latour, Bruno 13, 31
Leadbeater, Charles 3, 12, 23, 25, 26–28, 124, 137, 140, 145–146, 158–159, 160
leadership 2, 12–14
  modern 161–162
  moving to a different kind of 129–133
  leading collective change processes 131–133
  unlocking collective mindset 129–130
  and storytelling 65
learning forward 114–115
Learning Framework's Five Elements 125, *126*
learning organisms 115
  moving towards 129–133
learning questions 119
leverage points 12
Living Futures 101
loneliness, reducing 110–111, 112–113
long-term change in short-term world 67–70, 73, 75, 93
longing, concept of 32–33
Lyngaae, Uffe 161–162

M

Mannervik, Ulf 144
manufacturing industry, accelerating sustainable transition in 82–85
Manzini, Ezio 3, 5, 148
mapping and analysing systems 144–147
  hard and soft power 145–146
  'as is' before visualizing 'to be' 145
  an ongoing process 146–147
  positioning own organization in system 146
Mazzucato, Mariana 6–7, 76, 77, 141
McKinsey & Company 59–60
Meadows, Donella 11–12, 26
megaphone model of innovation 77–79, *78*
Melbourne Biodiversity Network (MBN) 167–173
  nested governance 169–171, *170*, 175
  Strategic Plan 168
mental health, reframing system around 47–50, 52–53
Merkel, Angela 95–96
mindset
  system 67
  tensions 60–66
    embracing the tension 61–63
    navigating in-between and both-and 63–66, *64*, *65*
  unlocking a collective 129–130
mission-oriented innovation 1, 6–8, 74–93
  creating directionality 74–75
  critical view 76–77
  driving commitment to change 75
  for long-term 75
  structuring portfolio 81–92
  top-down and bottom-up experimentation 76–81, *78*, **80**
mission washing 76–77
monitoring and evaluating structures 123–127
moon landing 6–7, 74, 76, 81
Mulgan, Geoff 17, 18, 19, 49, 179–180
multispecies design 66–67
Muratovski, Gjoko 148

N

navigation points xv
  navigating a new story 15–16, 52–53, 65, 86, 97, 100, 102, 146
  navigating balance 55–56, 57, 65, 92–93, 97, 100, 115, 124, 143, 171
  navigating experiments 65, 95–96, 97, 134–135
  navigating interdependence 65, 137–138, 175–176

Index

Nelson, Richard 76
nested governance 169–171, *170*, 175
Netherlands
 Concrete Agreement 154, 156
 Hestia project 28–29
network governance 153
New Nordic Cuisine movement 139–140
news, reading 19
Nietzsche, Friedrich 177
Norway, reducing loneliness among young students 110–111, 112–113
Nyby 166–167

O

Oldenburg, Ray 173–174
Organisation for Economic Cooperation and Development (OECD) 7, 10
 Observatory for Public Sector Innovation 75
 13 Reasons Why Missions Fail 76–77
 Innovation Portfolios 81–82
organization structures
 changing shape 133–134
 recomposing 173–175
orphan missions 77
Østergaard, Oskar Stokholm 25, 45, 46, 103
ownership struggle 171–173

P

Pagh, Christian 172
Panduro, Jesper 131
pathfinders xiv–xv
patient and impatient mindsets 60
Pedersen, David Budtz 114, 141
pessimism 18–19
philanthropy 162–164
place layers 169, *170*, 171, 175
a planetary perspective 66–67
playfulness and seriousness 103–107
 deep seriousness vs. deep playfulness 105, *106*
Polchar, Joshua 19
political decision making processes, dynamic learning in 127–129
Polman, Paul 68–69
polymers in liquid formulations (PLF), sustainable 86–88

portfolios
 approach to missions 80–81
 of experiments 113–114
 learning across 122
 structuring 81–92
  adaptive portfolios 82–85
  breaking down 88–90
  speculative portfolios 86–88
  theory of change 90–92, *90*
possibility thinking 88
power
 hard and soft 145–146
 letting go of 161–162
 within systems, changing 27
  Hestia project 28–29
preferred futures 45–53
 experimenting towards 100, 118
 integrating futures design and imagination 51–52
 seeing bigger picture 50–51
 Three Horizons Framework and 70–72, 89
 Vorby 47–50, 52–53
prototyping 111–114, 148
psychological safety 107–108
purpose, changing a system's 27

R

Raby, Fiona 9
Ramirez, Rafael 9, 42, 144
rational and speculative mindsets 60, 88
Realdania 163–164
'rebound effects' 59–60
relationships and system change 27–28
reporting
 company 68–69
 formats 127
resources and system change 27
retreaters 161–162
Rittel, Horst 23
Robertson, Brian J. 12–13
roles for systems change 158–162
Royal Society of Chemistry 86–88

S

scales
 learning at different 115–123
 tension in 59–60
scenario planning/development 9
scenius 139–140
Schjørring, Jakob 117–118

Schultz, Nikolaj 31
Selin, Cynthia 49
seriousness and playfulness 103–107
  deep seriousness vs. deep playfulness 105, *106*
'seven generation principle' 68
Sharpe, Bill 70, 71
short-term world, long-term change in 67–70, 73, 75, 93
Simon, Herbert 2, 5
SIT (Norwegian Student Welfare Organization) 110–111
Skagerak 131, 132
Skibsted, Jens Martin 63, 67
soft power 145–146
Søndergaard, Søren 164
speculative
  design 9
  portfolios 86–88
  and rational mindsets 60, 88
stakeholder groups 155–157
stars, birth of 177, 178
storytelling
  leadership and 65
  power of 15–16, 29, 50
strategic foresight 2, 9, 10
Striegler, Sara Gry 47, 48, 68, 69, 70, 79, 82, 113
Superflux 66–67
sustainers 155, 156
Sweden, Vinnova in 7–8, 75, 173, 175
system innovation 2, 11–12, 140
  connection to futures design 29
  four keys of 26–28
  in practice 28–29
system level learning 122–123
system mindset 67
system thinkers 26, 64–65
system traps 26
The Systemic Design Framework 64–66, *65*
systems acupuncture 89
systems, changing 25–29
systems theory 124–125, 142

T

tame problems vs. wicked problems **24**
technological solutions 19–20
tensions between opposing attitudes, holding, 57–73, 92–93
  image *58*
  a planetary perspective 66–67
  The Systemic Design Framework 64–66, *65*
  tension in mindset 60–66
  tension in scale 59–60
  tension in time 58–59
  Three Horizons Framework 70–73, *71*
  working for long-term change 67–70, 73, 75, 93
third spaces 173–174
Three Horizons Framework 70–73, *71*
  breaking down portfolio activities 89–90
time, tension in 58–59
tipping points 91–92
Tõnurist, Piret 75, 76, 81
traditional vs. mission-oriented innovation 79, **80**
transition brokers 157–158
transition design 3

U

unemployed, long-term 18
Unilever 68–69
  Sustainable Living Plan 69
United Nations Development Programme (UNDP) 124
University College Copenhagen 43

V

Vervoort, Joost 104–105, *106*
Vinnova 7–8, 75, 144, 173, 175
Vorby 47–50, 52–53, 102

W

Wales 69
Webber, M.M. 23, 24
WeDoDemocracy 67
well-being economy 33–34
  event at international conference 2024 105–107
Well-being of Future Generations Act, 2015 69
wicked problems 23–25
  vs. tame problems **24**
Wikipedia 159
wild problems 24
Winhall, Jennie 3, 5, 12, 23, 25, 26–28, 124, 137, 140, 145–146, 149–150, 158–159, 160, 177, 180–181

Winther Nielsen, Sigge 24, 48, 128
women, economic value of 34

Y

young people
  anxiety 18, 19, 48
  Hestia youth care project 28–29
  pervasive pessimism 19
  reducing loneliness among students 110–111, 112–113
  reframing system around mental health for 47–50, 52–53
  seeking influence and power 161–162
  transitioning from foster care to adulthood 116–123

www.ingramcontent.com/pod-product-compliance
Lightning Source LLC
Chambersburg PA
CBHW051543020426
42333CB00016B/2069